The Future of Biblical Archaeology

Dr. David Tee

Published by Dr. David Tee, 2020.

While every precaution has been taken in the preparation of this book, the publisher assumes no responsibility for errors or omissions, or for damages resulting from the use of the information contained herein.

THE FUTURE OF BIBLICAL ARCHAEOLOGY

First edition. July 29, 2020.

ISBN: 979-8201901219

Written by Dr. David Tee.

Table of Contents

About the Author

DR. DAVID TEE HAS SPENT over 25 years researching biblical archaeology and other archaeological topics. After spending 20 years in the working world after receiving his Bachelor of Theology degree Dr. Tee went back to school and pursued Church History and Biblical Archaeology degrees.

He has used his studies and experience to write on theological and archaeological subjects helping believers strengthen their faith. His www.theologyarchaeology.wordpress.com[1] website has been his main outlet over the past 8 years. Recently he added www.theoarch.wordpress.com[2] website to market his books and do some non theological writing.

---

1.   http://www.theologyarchaeology.wordpress.com

2.   http://www.theoarch.wordpress.com

Books by the Author
Noah's Flood Did Take Place: An Examination of the Non Scientific Evidence
Archaeology: What You need to Know
Archaeology and the Unwary Believer
Much to Talk About Vol. 1
Much to Talk About Vol. 2

BIBLICAL ARCHAEOLOGY has been under attack for many years now. There are far too many unbelievers involved in the field and they do not want that archaeological sub field overshadowing the people who also lived in the region.

• • • •

THE ISRAELITES WERE not the first group of people, but their lives intersect with the Biblical figures and have become a part of biblical archaeology whether anyone likes it or not. If it was not for the Bible, then no one would be interested in those groups of people nor would they invest so much money into digging up the many different sites that populate the promised Land.

• • • •

THOSE 'OTHER' GROUPS of people would be like the Mayan, the Aryans, the Germanic tribes, holding little interest of the modern archaeologist and scholar. While discoveries are made of these other nation's historical people, they do not bring debate, religious discussion or large wholesale changes to the understanding of any religious book like biblical archaeology does for the Bible.

• • • •

THAT IS WHERE THE BIBLICAL archaeologist comes in. He or she must must not let the influence of the unbelieving professional scholar or archaeologist to hide the truth of what occurred in the past.

• • • •

IF BIBLICAL ARCHAEOLOGY is to have a future then the biblical archaeologist must stand with God and let the world know that the

Bible is not wrong. It is said that archaeology and biblical archaeology does not prove the Bible true, yet that is exactly what those fields of research are doing as are many other research fields.

• • • •

THE BIBLICAL ARCHAEOLOGIST has some heavy responsibilities they have to shoulder if they want the truth to be told. They must point out the errors of those who do not accept the biblical record and set those mistakes straight.

• • • •

IT IS NOT AN EASY TASK because there is so much opposition to the Bible, the biblical record and the truth. In the following chapters the reality of both archaeology and biblical archaeology are shown. For the most part both fields of research are bind to the past as they lack specific information talking about historical events, cities, civilizations and people.

• • • •

ALSO, IF BIBLICAL ARCHAEOLOGY has a future, then it must separate itself from secular influence and redesign the field to follow God's admonitions, after all there are not escape clauses in God's word. Biblical archaeologists need to follow God's instructions over the instructions of secular science and archaeology.

• • • •

ONE OF THE MAIN PROBLEMS in this endeavor is that so many biblical archaeologists claim to be Christian yet their words, their theories and their conclusions only create confusion and lead many people away from the truthfulness of the Bible and its contents.

• • • •

THIS ATTITUDE IS SEEN in a variety of sectors in biblical archaeology as it is currently practiced. The locations of cities, the debates over who wrote the books of the Bible tend to undermine the faith of the normal Christian. As do the discussions on key issues like illiteracy or different key pieces of evidence which are re-dated to fit the accepted thinking of scholars and archaeologists.

• • • •

THE DIFFERENT CHAPTERS in this book take on a wide variety of topics to help the biblical archaeologist get on the right track and find some courage. They are not to please man but God even in this field of research.

• • • •

THE ARGUMENTS OF THOSE who do not believe are built on silence while God's word piles up pieces of physical evidence after physical evidence. It is only the assumptions, the conjecture, the leaps to conclusions and the hypothesis of the unbelieving archaeologist that claims the Bible to be in error.

• • • •

NEITHER ARCHAEOLOGY nor biblical archaeology make such claims. That is why it is up to the biblical archaeologist to take up the mantle and keep spreading the truth about the past.

• • • •

THE UNBELIEVING SCHOLAR or archaeologist won't do it. The verse 'so let your light shine before men' applies to the biblical archaeologist even as they participate in their chosen career. That light cannot shine if the biblical archaeologist is following the lead of the deceived, blind and lost unbelieving professional archaeologist or biblical scholar.

• • • •

IT MAY HAVE BECOME apparent that the term biblical archaeologist is being used equal with the term true Christian. That is because that is what a biblical archaeologist should be. He or she should be a true believer in God and his word.

• • • •

THAT IS THE ONLY WAY the truth of the past will come out and the only way the biblical archaeologist will find the truth. As Jesus said, the unbelieving world does not have the Spirit of Truth helping them only the follower of him.

• • • •

IF THE BIBLICAL ARCHAEOLOGIST wants the truth, then they need to be true believers and there is no other goal in biblical archaeology than to find the truth. Anything less does not help people or their faith.

• • • •

THERE IS A FUTURE FOR biblical archaeology but it is up to the decision of the biblical archaeologist if that future will be honest, fruitful, constructive and bring the truth. The faith of the people, in some ways, count on them to fulfill those duties.

• • • •

AS JESUS SAID, 'FEED my sheep'. That charge lies upon the shoulders of the biblical archaeologist as it does on the Christian preacher.

What is the Future of Biblical Archaeology

ITS A GOOD QUESTION

·····

IN HIS ARTICLE DISTINGUISHED Lecture in Archaeology: Communication and the future of American Archaeology Jeremy A. Sabloff posed a similar question but framed it in the words 'Will American archaeology survive in the twenty-first century?'

·····

HIS ANSWER TO HIS OWN question was of course it will. He was not so sure about his second question will it continue to thrive...? (#1). They are two very important questions Christians and Biblical archaeologists need to ask about biblical archaeology.

·····

I ASK THE QUESTION not because biblical archaeology is being attacked by unbelievers on a constant basis nor for the fact that it is slow to produce the physical results many believers want to see in order to continue in their faith.

·····

DUE TO THE LIMITATIONS of archaeology, both secular and biblical, as well as the lack of Christian archaeologists, Biblical Archaeology can only uncover so much. There must be a lot of patience when one wants to get more facts and information about our past.

·····

THE QUESTION WHAT IS the future of biblical archaeology is a serious one for Bible believers because that field is not over flowing with Christians digging up evidence proving the Bible true.

. . . .

INSTEAD IT IS FILLED with a majority of professionals who do not believe in either God or Jesus. Their work is influenced by their unbelief and that can pose a danger to biblical archaeology and the discoveries it uncovers.

. . . .

WHY SHOULD ANYONE CARE about ancient Israel

. . . .

AN ARCHAEOLOGY PROFESSOR teaching a class in Near Eastern Archaeology was asked the question by one of her first-year students the following question:

. . . .

WHY DO WE CARE ABOUT the origins of this small group of people anyway (#2)?

. . . .

THAT QUESTION WORKS hand in hand with the question what is the future of Biblical Archaeology. It reveals a mindset that biblical archaeologists are going to have to overcome if they want to have their work make an impact in the lives of young church adults, the church itself and the unbelieving world around them.

. . . .

A LOT OF PEOPLE DO not care about the history of modern-day Israel, they do not care about the lives and practices of the ancient Israelites and the do not care about the Bible.

• • • •

IT IS GOING TO BE A delicate and complicated task for biblical archaeologists to take on as their audience may be shrinking faster than they would like. Biblical archaeologists are going to have to stop assuming that people are going to be a willing audience if they cannot instill an attitude in their listeners that has them caring about the biblical past.

• • • •

THAT STUDENT'S QUESTION goes hand in hand with a statement made 50 years ago by John Fritz and Fred Plog when they wrote, "We suggest that unless archaeologists find ways to make their research increasing relevant to the modern world, the modern world will find itself increasingly capable of getting along without archaeologists" (#3).

• • • •

WHILE THAT PAIR OF archaeologists may have been talking about archaeology in general, it aptly applies to biblical archaeology as well. Biblical archaeologists need to make sure that their research is relevant to the individuals in the church whereby the latter can see how the information actually applies to their lives.

• • • •

FAILURE TO DO THAT means that many believers may ignore what the biblical archaeologists are doing and move on to something they feel is more relevant and worthwhile.

. . . .

SOME OF THE PROBLEMS in Biblical Archaeology

. . . .

IT IS THESE PROBLEMS that are helping the biblical archaeologists' audience in turning off what the biblical archaeologist has to say. These problems have arisen throughout the years as attitudes in the field of Biblical Archaeology has changed.

. . . .

IN THE OLD DAYS STICKING to discovering information about events, civilizations and people of the Bible led early biblical archaeologists to great discoveries. One example of this is the civilization of the Hittites. For over 1800 years historians and biblical scholars thought the biblical authors made up that civilization.

. . . .

YET WITH PERSISTENCE and a lot of hard work, the Hittite civilization was finally proven to be a reality and in the ancient era the biblical authors had it in. The lack of physical evidence is not a problem that is undermining the work of biblical archaeologists.

. . . .

IT IS AN ONGOING ISSUE that has been dealt with because God said, 'the just shall live by faith' & 'faith pleases God' (loose quote). While we can, are and will dig up physical evidence for different events, people and so on, our belief in Jesus is built on faith not physical evidence.

. . . .

PLUS, GOD IS NOT GOING to destroy what pleases him by overwhelming the world with physical evidence for everything recorded in the Bible. It is by faith that we are saved not physical evidence.

• • • •

ONE OF THE FIRST PROBLEMS that is influencing the field of Biblical Archaeology is the influence of unbelievers. Recently, Hershel Shanks the editor and founder of Biblical Archaeology Review retired and turned the control of his magazine over to an avowed atheist.

• • • •

THE CHANGE OF TONE in that magazine is already seen by some of the recent articles it has published since that change. This does not bode well for believers or those who look to BAR to be more independent in the ongoing archaeological debates and discussions between minimalists, maximalists, believers & unbelievers.

• • • •

THE NEXT PROBLEM THAT is influencing the field of Biblical Archaeology the wrong way is the growing number of people who either do not have any faith in God or have lost their faith because the field has not produced what they had hoped to find.

• • • •

TWO OF THE MORE WELL-known influences are Dr. William Dever and Dr. Bart Ehrman. Then, of course, there are a host of Jewish archaeologists who do not believe or accept the New Testament and their archaeological views are influenced by what they do or do not accept (#4).

• • • •

THE GROWING DISBELIEF alters the theories and explanations the biblical archaeologist reads, which in turn has some questioning the validity of the field of research as well as God and his authors.

. . . .

THE FINAL PROBLEM THAT will be discussed here is the one where the Christian archaeologist begin to contradict what the Bible says or promote theories or discoveries that do not coincide with the Biblical text.

. . . .

IN OTHER WORDS, THESE archaeologists are saying one thing and God is saying another. This takes its toll on the Christian and the non-Christian audience as well. If the Christian archaeologist does not agree with the Bible or stretches their theories and discoveries to make it seem like they agree with do yet do not in reality, then the audience begins to turn away from God and his word (#5).

. . . .

THESE ARE ONLY SOME of the problems that threaten the future of Biblical Archaeology. How long will the field survive and get the support of different nations and people if the very professionals who work in the field say something that God did not say?

. . . .

THESE PROBLEMS HAVE to be overcome if those hard working and honest biblical archaeologists are going to have their voice heard and the field to remain relevant to a modern generation.

. . . .

WHAT IS THE FUTURE of Biblical Archaeology

For the field of Biblical Archaeology to mean something changes have to be made. We read in the book of Acts that the new believers were of one mind and one heart (Acts 4:32).

• • • •

UNFORTUNATELY, THAT attitude has not made it successfully to the 21st century. There are many believing archaeologists who do not work well with each other and the reasons for that are many.

• • • •

GOD IS NOT THE AUTHOR of confusion thus the biblical archaeologists must get on the same page so the field can avoid embarrassing moments like when the Ark of Noah was supposedly discovered in 2010 (#6).

• • • •

THIS ONE MIND HAS TO be centered around the truth. Sadly, so many Christian archaeologists have adopted the secular scientific rules and frame their work under the influence of the unbeliever instead of God's word.

• • • •

JESUS SAID, 'YE SHALL; know the truth' and that the Spirit of truth is to guide the believer to that truth (John8:32 & 14:32ff). Secular scientific rules and methods avoid the truth in favor of asking questions, making up hypothesis among other attributes.

• • • •

SECULAR SCIENTIFIC guidance does not lead anyone to the truth because it does not have the Spirit of Truth guiding it. Instead it has the author of lies and deception as its leader. The believing scientist must avoid the influence of the secular scientific way or they are at risk of losing their faith as other scholars and biblical archaeologists have.

• • • • •

ALSO, BIBLICAL ARCHAEOLOGISTS have to be careful about what historical documents they accept. Reading into inscriptions and accepting only one-sided arguments by a civilization's enemies is not the way to get to the truth (#7).

• • • •

IT HAS TO BE REMEMBERED that most of the surviving historical documents were not written by Christians or following God or his Spirit of Truth. Their words must be analyzed in a biblical context keeping in mind God's instruction not to walk in the counsel of the ungodly (Psalm 1:1).

• • • •

THE WORDS DAVID WROTE in that Psalm apply to the field of Archaeology in all of its settings, especially Biblical Archaeology. Verse 6 of that Psalm is just as compelling and does not have an escape clause allowing for believing archaeologists to ignore God's instructions and walk in line with secular archaeological demands.

• • • •

ARCHAEOLOGY DOES NOT provide the whole historical story and the secular influence hides even more of it. To answer the question the future of biblical archaeology is bleak unless those involved in the field do not start following God and make the right changes.

• • • •

IS THERE A FUTURE FOR Biblical Archaeology

• • • •

YES, THERE IS. GOD wants his creation to know the truth and that desire leaves a wide opening for Christian Biblical Archaeologist to operate in. But they must do their archaeological work his way.

• • • •

CHRISTIAN ARCHAEOLOGISTS are often too worried about meeting the approval of the secular archaeologists. They want credibility and want their work published in the secular magazines and professional journals or status in their universities and so on.

• • • •

NOT ALL BUT TOO MANY and this desire interferes with their work and God using them to make an impact on the world. The secular world is not whom Christians archaeologists are to be pleasing or seeking any approval.

• • • •

THEIR WORK SHOULD BE seeking God's approval, containing the truth about the past and leading people to the validity of the Bible. God does not lie, and the Christian archaeologist cannot hide the truth from God's creation.

• • • •

THERE ARE TOO MANY people trying to hide the truth because they do not want to face the reality of the coming judgment and that their work was in vain. It is up to the Christian archaeologist to let their light shine in the Biblical Archaeology field.

• • • •

THIS LIGHT IS MORE than just sharing the gospel with their unbelieving counterparts, volunteers, and students. It includes doing Biblical Archaeology God's way and getting the whole story out.

• • • •

THAT WAY GOD IS NOT seen as a liar who makes things up to force people to believe in him. His word is also not seen as 'book of fairy tales written by Bronze Age goat herders.'

• • • •

INSTEAD THE BIBLE CAN be seen as what it really is, a very true book that has recorded actual history for all the world to come and know God.

• • • •

WORKS CITED

• • • •

#1. SABLOFF, J.A. (2013), "Distinguished lecture in archaeology", Annual Editions Archaeology, 10th edition, edited by MP Parker & E. Angeloni, pg. 23

#2. Anderson, R, (2020), Is Archaeology better off without religion", Aeon Rock of Ages, 2020, https://aeon.co/essays/is-archaeology-better-off-without-religion

#3. Op Cit Sabloff (2013)

#4. Calder, A., (2007), "Losing faith: how secular scholarship affects scholars", Creation Ministries Intl., https://creation.com/losing-faith-how-secular-scholarship-affects-scholars

#5. Collins, S., (2018), "Discovering the City of Sodom", Tell El-Hamman Excavation Project, https://tallelhammam.com/reports-%26-publications

#6. Chaffey, T., (2016), "Has the Ark Been Found?", Answers in Genesis, https://answersingenesis.org/noahs-ark/noahs-ark-found/has-ark-been-found/

#7. White, A., (2020), "Ancient Child Sacrifice and Abortion" Associates for Biblical Research, https://biblearchaeology.org/research/contemporary-issues/4623-ancient-child-sacrifice-and-abortion

Archaeology is Blind to the Past

WITHOUT A TIME MACHINE

• • • •

SCIENCE CANNOT TRULY see into the past. The relics it relies upon to create a picture of the world's history are mere artifacts that are vulnerable to modern human speculation (#1).

• • • •

THIS DOESN'T ONLY HOLD true for astronomy but for the other sciences as well, including archaeology. Most often the archaeologist is left only with a coin, a chair, or maybe a figurine to draw his or her conclusions from. Or all they have left are the eroding building foundations, blank walls, and empty rooms to speculate about the past.

• • • •

ARCHAEOLOGISTS ARE not fortunate enough to have contemporary ancient manuscripts uncover that detail the purpose, use or the reason for it being left where it was of anything they discover.

• • • •

THE ARCHAEOLOGIST MUST make up their own ideas about these things and more often than not, the theories they construct cannot be verified or even proven to be close to being true.

• • • •

LEAVING OUT THE MODERN world

• • • •

THERE ARE BASICALLY two approaches to looking at the ancient world from the modern perspective. There are those archaeologists who use the modern world, its thinking and human behavior to help them understand the past and those who don't.

· · · ·

FOR THE LATTER GROUP, the reasoning is that the ancient world did not have science helping them and were ignorant of many things. Supposedly, the ancients led a rather savage life and were not capable of thinking in modern terms (#2).

· · · ·

THIS THINKING FLIES in the face of the existence of men like Archimedes who was and is considered to be one of the greatest scientists of all time (#3). As it does to the Babylonian and other ancient astronomers who have been known to complicated astronomical calculations, observations and adjustments (#4).

· · · ·

THE ARCHAEOLOGISTS who follow the idea that the ancient world is separate from the modern world and the latter and do not use the modern world to help them understand the past also feel that God created two different kinds of people if they accept the fact that God created anything at all.

· · · ·

THEY LEAVE GOD OUT of the picture and ignore the Biblical references which show that the ancient world was filled with the same type of people that power the modern civilizations.

· · · ·

THE ANCIENTS HAD THEIR God given talents and intelligence. They also had emotions, desires and did not just eat, work, and pray, as some archaeologists would have the modern public believe.

• • • •

THEY ALSO INVENTED, committed crimes, had laws as well as more modern aspects that govern modern life.

• • • •

IT IS SAFE TO SAY THAT the modern world does help us define and understand the past. Those that take the opposite position willingly blind themselves to the reasons behind the ancients acted as they did.

• • • •

ONE REASON TO SAY THAT is that the modern world has societies all over the earth that still live like savages.

• • • •

ARCHAEOLOGY MAKES SOME wonderful discoveries

• • • •

THIS IT DOES VERY WELL. Archaeologists are known to uncover large buildings, ancient inscriptions and a host of personal artifacts that only give a peek into the lives of those who populated the ancient civilizations.

• • • •

ONE GREAT DISCOVERY showed that the ancient Babylonians had a social security system as well as time capsules. The people of that once great empire wanted future civilizations to know who they were, what they believed and what they saw as important (#5).

• • • •

IT IS ONLY DISCOVERIES like these that give us, as Paul said in Corinthians 13:12, an imperfect view of the past. We get little snippets that do not show us exactly how ancient life was conducted.

• • • •

ALL THE ARTIFACTS AND ancient structures only show a very tiny view of what the ancient world was like and if we are brave enough we can put those views together and see that the ancient world wasn't too much different from the modern one.

• • • •

PART OF THE REASON for that is that sin, evil and God are never changing and always present. Ancient men and women fall to lust, David and Bathsheba are an example of that sin, make mistakes, Moses and killing the Egyptian is an example of murder, and so many other non-biblical examples give us a very clear view that mankind has not changed in thousands of years.

• • • •

THE ANCIENT INSCRIPTIONS help clear up some of the mystery of the past by telling us how people though in different situations. Whether those inscriptions are accepted, rejected, or badly interpreted by modern scholars and archaeologists is not the point.

• • • •

THE POINT IS THESE inscriptions help provide a clearer view of what existed in ancient times. Tell Dan Stele is but one of those inscriptions which gives us evidence that the people of Israel and King David existed as the Bible says (#6).

• • • •

WE DO NOT GET MUCH about ancient Israel or other ancient civilizations because of the way these inscriptions are treated by modern scholars and archaeologists. The Behistun Inscription is another example of how ancient words are not totally accepted by modern scholars (#7).

• • • •

THE UNWILLINGNESS TO accept these inscriptions and other writings as they should be accepted help keep the past in the dark about ancient civilizations and people. The fact that many modern archaeologists do not accept the idea that the ancient world was literate helps to keep archaeology from seeing anything true about the past (#8).

• • • •

ITS A TEMPLE, NO ITS a goddess

• • • •

THIS IS A COMMON CRY by archaeologists. Far too many ancient building remains have been identified as temples even though there are no ancient manuscripts confirming the modern identification. The layout of the remains often leads archaeologists to make that identification even though there is no real reason for doing so.

• • • •

FOR EXAMPLE, THE EGYPTIAN temple at Karnak was expanding from its original size from about its original size built over 4,000 years ago. It is said that Pharaohs for over 2,000 years added their own sections to the building and modern Egyptologists and archaeologists call it a temple.

. . . .

YET, THE ANCIENT WORLD did not all believe in the ancient gods or participated in any religious activities. Plus, they needed other buildings to house criminals, their records, codexes, food supplies and so on. Even merchants needed a place to store their wares and sell them to the passing public.

. . . .

IN OTHER WORDS WHAT is declared a temple may not have been a temple and served some other useful purpose. Karnak may be one of the earliest examples of a museum not a temple. The description of the contents fit a description of a museum and not a temple (#9).

. . . .

THE SAME MENTALLY INFLUENCES the discovery of many ancient figurines. Far too many of these are interpreted to be depictions of ancient goddesses and it doesn't matter where in the world they are uncovered. The interpretation is basically the same even though other plausible reasons exist to explain so many figurines existing in the ancient world (#10).

. . . .

WOMEN HAVE NOT CHANGED over the centuries and it is highly possible, if not probable, that they had these figurines as knick knacks that decorated their walls, pieces of furniture and so on.

. . . .

NOT ALL WOULD BE GODDESSES, if any. Or the number of figurines could easily be the product or pottery class where many people were learning to make people as art. They were just not fortunate to have their best work survive to the modern age.

·····

IF THERE ARE MANUSCRIPTS linking these ancient figurines, they are few and far between. Even the great Mayan ceramic workshop discovered in 2018 does not come with manuscripts talking about the factory. It may have just been a warehouse and not related to any gods at all (#11).

·····

AT BEST, ARCHAEOLOGY does not know what these buildings and figurines were used for. Much of their modern descriptions on these ancient items are heavily influenced by their point of view and how low they view the ancient people.

·····

THERE ARE MANY CHURCHES, temples and knick knacks in the modern world yet very few people would say that the modern populations were religious or had artifacts of gods and goddesses in their home.

·····

THE LOSS OF INFORMATION

·····

THE MODERN UNINFORMED public may think that archaeological excavations are digging up vast amounts of information about the past. If one were to go by the overflowing museum storage rooms, they may have that view verified.

·····

YET, THE REALITY IS that very little of the ancient past is uncovered. Kenneth Kitchen described this loss of information in the first chapter of his book, 'The Bible In Its World' and the picture he painted was bleak not encouraging.

• • • • •

HE SAID THAT MOST SITES are eroding at a fast rate and that archaeologists, even after years of excavating at a site, only uncover between 2 and 5% of what was actually there (#12).

• • • • •

THAT MEANS THAT OVER the years since an archaeological site stopped being a real living village or city 95 to 98% of the past has been lost to the passing of time. Archaeology does not get a full picture of the past and much of the void is filled in with speculation, conjecture, assumption and leaps to conclusions.

• • • • •

UNFORTUNATELY, NO MATTER how deep the archaeologist digs, that information is lost forever. Archaeology cannot bring it back or reconstruct what actually took place.

• • • • •

ARCHAEOLOGY IS NOT to be relied on

• • • • •

THIS IS MORE FOR THE believer who may think that this one aspect or scientific research is going to uncover all the physical evidence they need to base their faith upon.

• • • • •

FAR TOO MANY BELIEVING archaeologists have stumbled and lost their faith when archaeological work has failed to provide that physical evidence they wanted to see. When applying archaeology and its finds to their faith and the Bible they see only a partial but very blind picture and make the wrong decision that the Bible is wrong.

• • • •

THESE ARCHAEOLOGISTS and other believers fail to apply the realities of archaeology, that it is a very limited field of study. They always end up deciding that science is right, and God is wrong.

• • • •

THEY DO NOT FACTOR in that the archaeologist may have dug in the wrong spot, left information buried in the dirt or that the physical evidence just didn't survive time and its destructive forces. They also didn't factor in what God said about his belief system.

• • • •

WITH THEIR MINDSET, influences by evil and other factors, they decide to leave God, Jesus, and their faith because science did not confirm what they believe. Instead of following God's words that the just live by faith and faith pleases him among other instructions, they follow the assumptions, etc., of unbelieving archaeologists and scholars and change to an unbeliever.

• • • •

ARCHAEOLOGY WILL TURN up some physical evidence to support the scriptures verifying accounts, civilizations, people and more but God will not let archaeology uncover so much that it destroys what pleases him.

• • • •

THE CHRISTIAN MUST follow God's words over those of archaeology and the hypothesis as well as the faulty conclusions archaeologists construct. Jesus told us about building on the sand and building upon the rock.

. . . .

BASING ONE'S BELIEFS on what archaeology and archaeologists claim took place would be building on the sand and that foundation is very weak. Believers need to use archaeology and the limited evidence it uncovers to help them build on the rock.

. . . .

THEY NEED TO SEE THAT God's word is true and that building on Jesus and God's word is building on the rock and that despite what any scientific field throws at them, their foundation and faith is solid because they believe God over man.

. . . .

WORKS CITED

. . . .

#1. WILLIAMS, A., & Hartnett, J., (2005), "Dismantling the Big Bang", Master Books green Forest AR.,

#2. Mal. S., (2019), "Paragraph on Ancient Age and Modern Age", Bangla Cyber, https://www.banglacyber.com/paragraph-on-ancient-age-and-modern-age/

#3. F.S. (2020) "Archimedes", Famous Scientists: The Art of Genius, https://www.famousscientists.org/archimedes/

#4. P.M., (2019), "A Brief History of Babylonian Astronomy", PsyMinds, https://psy-minds.com/babylonian-astronomy/

#5. Pellegrino, CR, (1995), "Return to Sodom and Gomorrah", William Morrow Paperbacks,

#6. BAS Staff, (2019), "The Tel Dan Inscription: The First Historical Evidence of King David from the Bible", Biblical Archaeology Society, https://www.biblicalarchaeology.org/daily/biblical-artifacts/the-tel-dan-inscription-the-first-historical-evidence-of-the-king-david-bible-story/

#7. Mark, JJ, (2019), "Behistun Inscription", Ancient History Encyclopedia, https://www.ancient.eu/Behistun_Inscription/

#8. Dever, WG, (2009), "How Archaeology Illuminates the Bible", Biblical Archaeology Society, Lectures on 2 CDs

#9. Jarus, O. (2012), "Karnak: Temple Complex of Ancient Egypt", Live Science, https://www.livescience.com/25184-karnak-temple.html

#10 Cowiw, A., (2019), "Largest Ever Maya Figurine Workshop Discovered Accidentally in Unexplored Mound", Ancient Origins, https://www.ancient-origins.net/news-history-archaeology/maya-figurine-workshop-0011782

#11 Ibid

#12 Kitchen, K./, (2004), "The Bible In Its World". Wipf & Stock,

Is Archaeology an Ally of the Bible

INTRODUCTION

. . . .

IN DETERMINING IF THERE is a future for biblical archaeology it must first be determined the role of archaeology in the biblical studies and examination of the Bible. Then to be able to determine that role, the identity of archaeology must be determined as there are many scholars and archaeologists who disagree with the term Biblical Archaeology. Their opposition can be seen in the following words: Scholars disagree about whether we can speak of "biblical archaeology." Some say that archaeology is archaeology—that is, its methods and goals are essentially the same everywhere, whether the Bible is involved or not. They also have valid concerns about the unscientific (occasionally even fraudulent) claims that have been perpetrated in the name of "biblical" archaeology. They believe we should use another term, such as "Palestinian archaeology," or speak of "archaeology and the Bible."

Perhaps the term biblical archaeology has fallen into disfavor because scientists today are simply not very interested in biblical matters. Scholars with a professional interest in the Bible are not as actively engaged in archaeological work as they once were. Today, professional archaeologists study a broad spectrum of cultural and anthropological interests that may not be immediately relevant for the student of the Bible. The long-standing alliance between biblical studies and archaeology is not as firm as it once was. (#1).

. . . .

IT IS A MUST THAT BIBLICAL Archaeology remain labeled with those terms as there are more people interested in the Bible than there are those of the Palestinian people or other people groups who occupied the Levant. It is the Bible that brings the message of hope not any ancient people group.

. . . .

FOR THIS CHAPTER AND book the label Biblical Archaeology will be used in its traditional sense and be restricted to archaeology that concerns the Bible, its contents, and people. There can be no change to its label in spite of what scholars and archaeologists want to see happen.

. . . .

BIBLICAL ARCHAEOLOGY is important because it helps keep the field clear of confusion and aids in keeping a future for that field of research. With that foundation, the role of Biblical Archaeology can be better determined. The role will help create a direction for those participating in the field and help separate the fact from the fiction.

. . . .

THE MODERN ROLE OF Biblical Archaeology

. . . .

PAUL MAIER WROTE A paper some years ago about archaeology being a friend or a foe to the Bible and in its opening paragraph, he states that the Christian over the years has assumed that archaeology and its discoveries will ultimately support the biblical record. (#2).

. . . .

THIS HAS BEEN THE TRADITIONAL view of the church when it comes to Biblical archaeology. There have been many people over the past 200 to 250 years who have spent vast fortunes looking for physical evidence for the biblical record.

• • • •

THEIR EFFORTS HAVE been well rewarded as museums around the world have been filled with artifacts relating to biblical nations, civilizations, main figures in biblical accounts and so on. This is a very important role as there are too many scholars and archaeologists who have decided not to believe in Jesus out there making all sorts of claims about the Bible, God and the biblical records.

• • • •

SOME OF THESE MEN AND women belong to a group called the minimalist who are known to deny any historicity of much of the Old Testament. Even deny the historicity of Abraham and the patriarchs, the Israelite sojourn in Egypt, the Exodus, and Joshua's conquest of the Promised Land. They further question whether David and Solomon ever existed, at least as the powerful sovereigns described in the Old Testament (#3).

• • • •

THAT BRINGS ON ANOTHER role for Biblical Archaeology. This field of research has to be the standard in which the unbelieving archaeologist and scholars are kept honest in their work. The information uncovered by believing scholars and archaeologists can counter what their unbelieving counterparts claim.

• • • •

WITHOUT THIS FIELD of research being able to do its job and perform as expected, then much of history, not just biblical history would be lost. Not because it did not happen but because the unbeliever has been able to hide the documentation, reassign evidence and basically say that archaeology supports their views and not God's.

• • • •

BIBLICAL ARCHAEOLOGY in this case is an ally to the Bible as it helps keep the truth from being hidden from those who need it- the people.

• • • •

IS ARCHAEOLOGY AN ALLY to the Bible

• • • •

IT GOES WITHOUT SAYING that whether one calls the field of research Archaeology or Biblical Archaeology it is an ally to the Bible. This is not said because the participants are biased in favor of the biblical record.

• • • •

BUT BECAUSE THE TERM Biblical Archaeology is targeting the peoples, events and civilizations that are found in the Biblical record. The definition of the combine term says:

• • • •

BIBLICAL ARCHAEOLOGY encompasses archaeological investigations of cultures and peoples described in Jewish and Christian religious texts (including the Old Testament, Apocrypha, and New Testaments) from roughly 3200 BC to the first century AD. It combines archaeological investigations with textual analysis to aid in understanding everyday life and events from the time. (#4).

• • • •

THE BIBLE NEEDS ITS own archaeological research field because, as has been the complaint of many archaeologists over the years, there are few extra biblical documents that talk about biblical events, people, and civilizations.

• • • •

TO SEE THE REALITY of the complaints all you have to do is read about the Israelite sojourn in and exodus and see how the Egyptian records and the records of neighboring countries do not record this vital event in Hebrew history. Thus, Biblical Archaeology becomes a great ally to the Bible as its research searches for the evidence for those recorded events (#5).

• • • •

IF THE ARCHAEOLOGIST limits his or her work to the discoveries of the secular records, then they would miss out on much of the past and comes to the conclusion that the Bible is not true.

• • • •

BY USING THE BIBLE to guide archaeologists, and this has been done since biblical archaeology was originally used in the 17th and 18th centuries., searchers were able to find numerous biblical cities throughout the Holy Land as well as other artifacts and records that showed the Hebrews were not the figment of someone's imagination.

• • • •

AT LEAST TILL THE 8TH century BC where other archaeological records have shown that the Assyrian assault and the Babylonian exile were conducted on historical people called the Israelites. That leaves the problem of King David but with a 1993 discovery by Avraham Biran. King David is shown to have existed (#6).

• • • •

EVEN WITH ARCHAEOLOGY an ally of the Bible the critics to its historical record do not remain silent and think of many ways to discredit the discoveries. They either claim the inscription of King

David's name is a forgery or mistranslated. Or they remain silent on how a supposed mythical people suddenly became an actual society that was a threat to surrounding kingdoms (#7).

· · · ·

ARCHAEOLOGY IS INDEED an ally whether it is the general field of Archaeology or its subset Biblical Archaeology. There have been enough discoveries in both categories to show that the Bible is not some work of fiction. As Clifford Wilson says

· · · ·

IT IS INDEED TRUE THAT very often archaeology does endorse particular Bible happenings. Some would say that in this way it "proves the Bible", though such a statement should be taken with reservation since it is far too sweeping. There are many thousands of facts in the Bible which, of course, are not capable of verification, because the required evidence has long since been lost. However, it is remarkable that where true confirmation is possible, the Bible withstands investigation in a way that is unique in all literature. This is not to say that viewpoints about the Bible have never changed because of archaeological findings (#8).

· · · ·

THIS STATEMENT IS SUPPORTED by what Dr, Nelson Glueck stated about archaeology and the discoveries made by archaeologists:

· · · ·

AS A MATTER OF FACT, however, it may be clearly stated categorically that no archeological discovery has ever controverted a single biblical reference. Scores of archeological findings have been made which confirm in clear outline or exact detail historical statements in the Bible (#9).

• • • •

THAT RECORD HAS NOT changed in the time between now and when he said it. There has still been no archaeological discovery that disproves the Bible. So yes, Archaeology and Biblical Archaeology are the allies of the Bible.

• • • •

WHY CAN'T WE FIND EVIDENCE for Kings David & Solomon

• • • •

AS MENTIONED EARLIER, we do have some evidence for King David. The Tel Dan Stele is just one inscription that mentions the name David and in recent years Dr. Eilat Mazar has made her own discoveries concerning both David and Solomon (#10).

• • • •

YET, WE MAY NOT FIND more specific information about David and Solomon. The city of Jerusalem has actually been destroyed and rebuilt over 15 times. That amount of change is bound to destroy any real evidence we could have had about both Kings (#11).

• • • •

THIS IS THE ISSUE AS minimalists and other skeptics do not allow for this limitation when it comes to archaeology and the Bible. They will allow it for other civilizations and authors of books but not the Bible.

• • • •

TO THEM, IF THERE IS no archaeological evidence then in their minds the event did not take place and the people did not exist. This is said very clearly by the late Phillip Davies in his lecture for a biblical Archaeology Society lecture series in the late 90s. He flat out said that it did not happen (#12).

• • • •

THIS IS THE STRUGGLE that the biblical archaeologist has. While Biblical Archaeology and its parent Archaeology are allies to the Bible, the professionals in the field can be very antagonistic towards what is uncovered as well as the biblical record.

• • • •

THE ADVERSARY OF THE Bible

• • • •

AS HAS BEEN SHOWN BIBLICAL Archaeology and Archaeology are the allies to the Bible and its record. But that doesn't mean there is no opposition to the record the bible contains.

• • • •

EVEN THOUGH THE DISCOVERIES eventually are shown to be supportive the Bible still has an opponent questioning and dismissing its contents and validity. It is not the discovery of an artifact, building or other ancient find that opposes the Bible.

• • • •

THESE DISCOVERIES ARE often mute and are victim to the unbelief of those making the discovery. Thus, it is not the discovery of the item itself that brings the opposition but the lack of belief of the professional making the discovery.

• • • •

IT IS THEIR ASSUMPTIONS, leaps to conclusions, conjectures and even hypothesis that claim the bible is wrong. It is not the discovery making that claim. Those assumptions, etc., are created by the deception and blindness in the lives of those professionals who do not believe in Christ and which originate with evil.

• • • •

AS THE BIBLE REMINDS us that our enemy is not of this world nor is it human sourced. The unbelieving archaeologist and bible scholar are merely the tool being used to help deceive the rest of the world.

• • • •

THE BELIEVER MUST KEEP this fact in mind when dealing with those who do not believe. Without this influence it may be easier for them to see the truth and how great an ally Biblical Archaeology is to the Bible.

• • • •

WORKS CITED

• • • •

#1. PACKER, J. I., TENNEY, M. C., & White, W., Jr. (1997). Nelson's illustrated manners and customs of the Bible (p. 65). Nashville, TN: Thomas Nelson.

#2. Maier, P., (2004), "Archaeology: Ally or Adversary of the Bible" Christian Research Journal, volume 27, number2, retrieved from http://www.equip.org/PDF/DA111.pdf

#3. Ibid

#4. Cheggs Study, (2020), retrieved from https://www.chegg.com/homework-help/definitions/biblical-archaeology-51

#5. Tee, DT, (2017), "What is the Evidence for the Israelite Sojourn?", Theologyarchaeology, retrieved from https://theologyarchaeology.wordpress.com/2017/07/07/what-is-the-evidence-for-the-israelite-sojourn/

#6. Op Ct MaierP., (2004)

#7. Ibid

#8. Wilson, C. A. (1972). Does Archaeology Prove the Bible? Bible and Spade, 1(1), 3.

#9. Nelson Glueck, Rivers in the Desert, (New York: Farrar, Strous and Cudahy, 1959), 136.

#10 PBS, The Bible's Buried Secrets: The Palace of King David, retrieved from https://www.pbs.org/wgbh/nova/bible/mazar.html

#11 Op Cit Maier, P., (2004)

#12 Lecture Phillip Davies 1998 BAS

There Are No Escape Clauses

EVEN FOR BIBLICAL ARCHAEOLOGISTS

. . . .

THIS PERTAINS TO THE instructions God has given everyone. In the Bible both God and Jesus laid out their instructions and told their followers what they must do. In none of those verses we find no escape clause excluding or permitting the biblical archaeologist from carrying out those directives.

. . . .

IN OTHER WORDS, A BIBLICAL archaeologist must follow God's way as they do their work regardless of the rules and demands set down by secular scholars and archaeologists. There is no verse allowing the believing archaeologist to follow the unbelieving rules over God's instructions.

. . . .

THIS INCLUDES DEFYING the scientific method when it calls for such behavior. The secular scientific method is not adequate and often fails to do a proper job. Even though archaeology is described as being a science and the same methods are supposed to be used, those methods and scientific structure do not trump God's instructions and rules (#1).

. . . .

THIS CHAPTER WILL OUTLINE as many of God's instructions to Biblical Archaeologists in order to help guide them when they do their work. The believing archaeologist is not required to please the unbelieving professional.

• • • •

BUT THEY ARE REQUIRED to please God and God has, through Samuel, said that 'to obey is better than to sacrifice' (1 Sam. 15:22) (#2). The rules of God always trump the rules of man and if the Biblical Archaeologist wants to find the truth, please God and make an impact for him, then their priority should be in implementing His rules and direction into their professional lives.

• • • •

GOD IS NOT GOING TO punish the Biblical Archaeologist if the secular counterpart is upset and gets angry. As long as the Biblical Archaeologist honestly follows his rules and follows them correctly. That means that the Biblical Archaeologist needs better understanding of God's word when applying it to their lives and interaction with other professionals.

• • • •

GOD'S INSTRUCTIONS are not limited to just personal aspects of life. They apply to all professionals, all businesses and even governments and their officials. If they didn't then they would not be God's word and something else would rule over God. Letting that happen is wrong and heresy.

• • • •

THE ULTIMATE GOAL OF the Biblical archaeologist is to bring glory to God, and they cannot do that if they shy away from following God and turn to the rules of unbelievers to guide their work.

• • • •

MAKING AN IMPACT FOR God through biblical archaeology is just one option the Christian has available to them. It is a great field to

let their let shine for God on a dark world as even Biblical Archaeology
has its dark spots.

• • • •

GOD'S INSTRUCTIONS to the Biblical Archaeologist

• • • •

THERE IS NO SPECIAL or unique order to the following
instructions. Just read them with an open heart and ask God to point
things out in your lives that need fine tuning or change.

• • • •

#1. COLOSSIANS 3:9- Do not lie to one another, since you laid aside
the old self with its evil practices.

• • • •

CREATING A HYPOTHESIS is not necessarily a lie. It is a point of
direction for the archaeologist to follow. When it becomes a lie is when
the archaeologist finds that hypothesis is not correct yet hides the truth
from everyone who reads and uses his words.

• • • •

THE BIBLICAL ARCHAEOLOGIST needs to realize that they are
not speaking to just anyone when they publish their work, write their
articles and books, or do their lectures. If their information is not true,
then they will be lying to their fellow believers.

• • • •

BUT LYING IS NOT JUST continuing to use the same hypothesis or
theory, it is also found in promoting the wrong location for biblical and

other cities, towns, or events. One such event would be Noah's Flood, and another would be the Exodus.

· · · ·

JUST BECAUSE THERE is little evidence found that satisfies the unbeliever's demands does not mean those events did not happen. Lying to one's fellow believers come sin when the Biblical Archaeologist agrees with the unbeliever and declares that God is wrong because there is no physical evidence supporting the biblical record.

· · · ·

GOD DOES NOT LIE THUS the Biblical Archaeologist must get on God's side and say that those events took pace in spite of the lack of evidence. If he or she does not they are influencing other believers to doubt God and end up disbelieving him in other areas of the Bible or walking away from their faith.

· · · ·

#2. 1 PETER 4: 11- WHOEVER speaks, is to do so as one who is speaking the utterances of God; whoever serves is to do so as one who is serving by the strength which God supplies; so that in all things God may be glorified through Jesus Christ, to whom belongs the glory and dominion forever and ever. Amen.

· · · ·

PETER'S WORDS ARE BACKED up by what Paul said in 1 Cor. 10:31 and his words go as follows "Whether, then, you eat or drink or whatever you do, do all to the glory of God."

· · · ·

IN BOTH VERSES THE key words are put in bold to highlight the fact that there are no escape clauses in God's word. Biblical Archaeology conducted by Biblical Archaeologists must bring glory to God and that cannot be done when the Biblical Archaeologist strays from God's word and practices secular instruction in favor of God's.

* * * * *

ONE CANNOT BRING GLORY to God by publishing or lecturing with misinformation, false information or information that does not lead the reader or listener to the truth and the correct answers.

* * * * *

A GOOD QUESTION THE Biblical Archaeologist can ask themselves is if their writings, conclusions, lectures will bring glory to God or will it lie to the people.

* * * * *

#3. PSALM 1:1- HOW BLESSED is the man who does not walk in the counsel of the wicked, Nor stand in the path of sinners, Nor sit in the seat of scoffers!

* * * * *

THE FELLOW PROFESSIONAL archaeologist and bible scholar participating in Biblical archaeology may be really nice people, friendly, intelligent and knows their archaeology but if they are not true believers, their counsel is not what you should seek or follow.

* * * * *

ONCE YOU START TO FOLLOW their words and ideas, you stop following God's and that is not going to lead you to the truth nor will it bring reward or help from God. The archaeologist may even be a good friend, but counsel needs to come from true godly people.

• • • •

THE UNBELIEVING ARCHAEOLOGIST or scholar is deceived and does not have the Spirit of Truth helping them. They cannot know the truth or how to get to it and their words need to be taken with a grain of salt as well as ignoring them.

• • • •

THIS INSTRUCTION DOES not mean that the true Biblical Archaeologist cannot offer advice, counsel, and instruction to their unbelieving counterparts. The unbelievers have no such instruction preventing them from hearing your words of advice.

• • • •

IF YOU KNOW THE BETTER way, then you should speak out and be the wise voice of reason instead of being sidetracked into pursuing dead end leads that waste time and resources.

• • • •

GOD KNOWS WHERE THE information is and if you need an example, Dr. Bryant Wood's research at Jericho, with God's help, led him to the evidence that proves that Kathleen Kenyon was wrong in her conclusions that Jericho did not exist at the time of the conquest (#3).

• • • •

IF ONE WALKS IN THE counsel of the ungodly, they would agree with Kenyon and dismiss the Biblical event as not being true. They would also miss out on a lot of ancient information that leads one to the knowledge that the Bible is true.

• • • •

#4. I CORINTHIANS 10:24a- Let no one seek his own good, but that of his [i]neighbor.

• • • •

THIS MAY SEEM LIKE an odd instruction that the Biblical Archaeologist needs to follow but it is a very important instruction to help other believers spiritually. The work that the Biblical Archaeologist should be doing is not to be done solely for their own benefit.

• • • •

THE BIBLICAL ARCHAEOLOGIST must examine their conclusions, theories and other archaeological work and see how it will benefit the believer in the church. The Biblical archaeologist is not working just to uncover the past but working hard to build the faith in those Christians who depend on what the Biblical Archaeologists uncover to help them in their walk with God.

• • • •

IT IS A VERY TOUGH responsibility, but it cannot be done by anyone else. The unbelieving archaeologist or scholar is not going to do this. They would rather claim that the Bible is not true so they can avoid its teaching and not worry about the final judgment.

• • • •

THE BIBLICAL ARCHAEOLOGIST is placed in that position by God so that they can get the right information to God's people and the rest of creation. The truth must be told not just to keep the unbelieving professionals honest, but to make sure that God's human creation does not lose faith in him and side with evil.

. . . .

#5. MATTHEW 7:1- DO not judge so that you will not be judged

. . . .

THIS CAN HAPPEN A LOT when Biblical Archaeologists decide that they do not like what they have found about ancient societies. Their failure to adhere to this command leads them to sin and possibly condemn people who did no wrong.

. . . .

NO MATTER WHAT EVIL practices the ancient people followed and what gods they worshiped, they are no lesser God's creation than the Biblical Archaeologist or the people in the church he or she is sending his information to through their different means.

. . . .

LEADING GOD'S PEOPLE to judge and condemn long dead people is still violating that command and leading them to sin. That is not the task the Biblical Archaeologist is to do. Instead they are to help the modern believer learn how to look at the information correctly without passing judgment on the ancient unbelieving civilizations.

. . . .

IT MUST BE REMEMBERED by both groups that the modern world has not seen the end of those who worship other gods or practice evil on a daily basis. If one wants their message to make an impact for God, then one cannot be caught judging the ancient societies.

• • • •

#6. PSALM 25: 4 & 5- Make me know Your ways, O Lord; Teach me Your paths.

Lead me in Your truth and teach me, For You are the God of my salvation.

• • • •

THE BIBLICAL ARCHAEOLOGIST must be humble and have God as their teacher. After all it is not the Biblical Archaeologist's world that they are excavating. They are digging into God's world and God's events and people.

• • • •

THIS FACT SHOULD MOTIVATE the Biblical Archaeologist to make sure they are not placing themselves above God in their work or their conclusions. God is the only one who knows the past and what really went on. It is impossible for the Biblical archaeologist to know what took place in ancient times without God's help.

• • • •

THAT FACT SHOULD HUMBLE the Biblical archaeologist and drive them to place themselves under God's direction not their own. Being humble makes it easier for the Biblical archaeologist to be honest and not lie about or misrepresent the past.

• • • •

PUTTING GOD FIRST AND submitting to his superior position sets a great example for the people in the churches and the cities of the world. It also helps the message that the Biblical archaeologist brings to be heard. One is not representing themselves or their work but representing God and what he knows took place in the past.

. . . .

#7. 1 COR. 13: 1- IF I speak with the tongues of men and of angels, but do not have love, I have become a noisy gong or a clanging cymbal.

. . . .

LOVE IS WHAT SHOULD be driving the Biblical Archaeologist. Their love for God, their love for the truth and their love for the people they are going to be sharing their words with whether directly or indirectly.

. . . .

GETTING ONE'S MESSAGE across depends on love. Archaeology is no time to feel or be superior to one's fellow believer, The field may be full of adventure and excitement, but it is no better or greater than any other field of research or industry.

. . . .

THE BIBLICAL ARCHAEOLOGIST should feel more honored that God has chosen them to participate in the field and work hard to protect his people. They should let God's love flow through them so that they have the right attitude when sharing what they have discovered.

. . . .

SEEING GOD'S PEOPLE protected with the truth is an honorable task and should not be taken lightly. Plus, that love needs to come through when presenting the material if one wants to make the right impact for God.

. . . .

THE PEOPLE MUST KNOW that they are not being treated like children and only love elevates them to being equals.

· · · ·

#8. ZECHARIAH 4:6- THEN he said to me, "This is the word of the Lord to Zerubbabel saying, 'Not by might nor by power, but by My Spirit,' says the Lord of hosts.

· · · ·

THIS IS THE SAME FOR Biblical Archaeology. It is not by the strength of the archaeologist or the biblical scholar that the truth about the past is being uncovered. It is by the grace of God and his power that reveals to Biblical Archaeologists where to dig, how deep to go and so on.

· · · ·

THE BIBLICAL ARCHAEOLOGIST must rely on God if they are going to succeed and help God's people stay strong in the faith.

· · · ·

A COUPLE OF MINOR POINTS

· · · ·

FIRST, THE BIBLICAL archaeologist must be aware of and acknowledge the weakness of the research field they are participating in. Archaeology, no matter which version, will not be able to find all the physical evidence people demand to see.

· · · ·

THE REASON FOR THAT is that God requires people to have faith. Hebrews 11:6 says 'And without faith it is impossible to please Him, for he who comes to God must believe that He is and that He is a rewarder of those who seek Him.'

• • • •

ARCHAEOLOGY DOES NOT exist to provide everyone with all the physical evidence they want in order to believe God and in his son. Faith will always be part of the equation even in the field of Biblical archaeology.

• • • •

WHILE GOD GIVES EVERYONE enough physical evidence to shore up their faith, he will not provide so much that their faith is ruined. God does not destroy what pleases him.

• • • •

THUS, THE BIBLICAL Archaeologist cannot be an idealist but use all of God's word to protect them when the research fails to produce the evidence they seek.

• • • •

SECOND, THE BIBLICAL Archaeologist cannot leave information in the ground. This is a common ideology held by many archaeologists as they feel the future may bring new techniques and tools to help discern the data surrounding the different discoveries (#4).

• • • •

LEAVING INFORMATION in the ground is foolish as there is no guarantee the future will bring those tools or techniques. There is also no certainty that there will be a future at a given excavation.

• • • •

IT IS BEST TO UNCOVER all the information so that nothing is lost, and a fuller picture of the past can be constructed. The Biblical archaeologist must get to the truth and they cannot do that by leaving discoveries buried in the ground.

. . . .

WORKS CITED

. . . .

#1. SCIENCE DAILY (2020), "Archaeology", retrieved from https://www.sciencedaily.com/terms/archaeology.htm

#2. All scriptures quoted in this chapter will be taken from the New American Standard Bible (NASB) Copyright © 1960, 1962, 1963, 1968, 1971, 1972, 1973, 1975, 1977, 1995 by The Lockman Foundation

#3. Wood, B, (2008), "The Walls of Jericho", Associates for Biblical Research, retrieved from https://biblearchaeology.org/research/conquest-of-canaan/3625-the-walls-of-jericho?highlight=WyJqZXJpY2hvIiwiamVyaWNobydzIiwiamVyaWNob

#4. Callaway,, JA, (1979) "Dame Kathleen Kenyon 1906-1978," The Biblical Archaeologist, Vol. 42, No. 2., pp. 122-125.

THERE IS ALWAYS A LITTLE doubt

• • • •

WHEN IT COMES TO THE Bible, there are a lot of people who accept it as the word of God. Then there are those who do not know who wrote it and those who reject the fact that God wrote the Bible through human authors.

• • • •

SOME OF THE LATTER two groups will provide a variety of different answers as they say God, some scholars or even some people. A lot of people in this world just do not know who actually wrote the bible. What makes the problem even worse that there are a lot of scholars just refuse to give any divine aspect to the Bible and claim that Moses could not have written the first 5 books because he and the Hebrews were illiterate. One scholar went as far as to say that the texts meant nothing to the Hebrews till about the 8th century (#1).

• • • •

THE ARGUMENT OF ILLITERACY is just one of many reasons why scholars reject the traditional and correct view of the authors of the different books of the Bible. The idea that the texts meant nothing to the Hebrews, as is the idea of illiteracy, is made without any real evidence whatsoever.

• • • •

JUST BECAUSE THE PEOPLE disobeyed the Hebrew Bible does not mean that the texts meant nothing to them and that their fellow citizens did not put their faith in its words. Then the suggestion that

Moses was illiterate flies in the face of what Jesus said in John 5: 46 in that Moses wrote about Him.

• • • •

WHAT FOLLOWS IS AN examination of some of the arguments used to discredit God and his human authors.

• • • •

WHAT THE SCHOLARS SAY

• • • •

IN THIS SECTION, WHAT the scholars claim will be made in block quotes and then addressed underneath. The sources will be in the work cited page with the quotes following the 1,2, 3... system as they will be listed in order of use.

• • • •

SET ASIDE WHAT RELIGIOUS tradition says, and discover who wrote the Bible according to the scholars who have examined the actual evidence (#2).

• • • •

THIS IS ONE OF THE keys to the whole argument against the traditional view of biblical authorship. The author of that quote states that the scholars have examined the actual evidence yet, in the article he does not lay out in an organized fashion exactly what that evidence is.

• • • •

THE AUTHOR MAKES A lot of declarations that the titled authors did not actually do the writing but does not point to any significant physical evidence showing those declarations are right. He does delve into the Documentary Hypothesis but that will be discussed later. He sheds absolutely no light on who he thinks actually wrote those biblical books. The same goes for the NT as he cites the standard argument that the authors only used key names to get their words read or that they used the imaginary Q as their source.

· · · ·

HIS ARGUMENTS ARE UNDONE by the following words found near the beginning of his article:

· · · ·

BUT GIVEN ITS IMMENSE reach and cultural influence, it's a bit surprising how little we really know about the Bible's origins. (#3).

· · · ·

SCHOLARS DO NOT HAVE any evidence that explicitly or indirectly counters the traditional view of who wrote the biblical books. They will find alternative aspects that they try to manipulate as the following quote shows.

· · · ·

BUT GOOD CHRISTIAN scholars of the Bible, including the top Protestant and Catholic scholars of America, will tell you that the Bible is full of lies, even if they refuse to use the term. And here is the truth: Many of the books of the New Testament were written by people who lied about their identity, claiming to be a famous apostle — Peter, Paul or James — knowing full well they were someone else. In modern parlance, that is a lie, and a book written by someone who lies about his identity is a forgery (#4).

· · · ·

WHETHER THEY ARE GOOD Christian scholars or not is an argument for another day. What is important is that according to Dr. Ehrman, they and he think the biblical authors lied about who they were as their names did not have the name recognition to be included in the Bible.

• • • • •

YET, ONCE AGAIN, DR. Ehrman and these scholars do not produce real evidence that these actual authors lied. They use the existence of other works which fall under that category and then claim that God's authors sinned to get his word to his people.

• • • • •

THAT IS RIDICULOUS and there is no way these men and women can produce any evidence to prove their case. Once people found out that the author was not who he said he was, then those people would dismiss his words and look for other books they could use as scripture. The forged works would not be included in holy writings because everyone would know that they were false.

• • • • •

THE SCHOLARS WHO MAKE this argument, have not thought things through very well. They have a low regard for the intelligence of the ancient people and remove characteristics from their abilities just to make sure the supposed evidence fits their argument.

• • • • •

SCHOLARS INCREASINGLY acknowledge the possibility of a cultural gap between the ancient Israelite masses whose villages we excavate, on the one hand, and the literate, urban elite that wrote the Hebrew Bible, on the other. If the intellectuals who wrote the Bible largely ignored the existence of demons, then they must have had another way to account for and control fortune and misfortune (#5).

. . . .

THIS IS A SIMILAR ARGUMENT to the illiterate one. The only difference here is that it is the elites who are literate and fashioned the biblical texts after their own purposes. The argument progresses that the elites were trying to control the masses and keep them under some sort of bondage, similar to what cults do today and have done throughout history.

. . . .

AGAIN, THE ARGUMENT for illiteracy does not hold up as there is no way to prove that the common Hebrews did not read or write. Saying there were no schools for their children to attend does not mean that schools for their children did not exist. Or that education was not conducted by the parents, friends, or relatives.

. . . .

LIKE ALL ARGUMENTS against the authorship of the bible, this one is impossible to prove as true because there is no evidence supporting this thinking. What proves the argument untrue is that if this scenario did take place, what would stop God from raising someone up and exposing the false hood and have the scriptures rewritten?

Also, once the people found out that their scriptures were fake, why would they follow them? Most likely the people would rebel and seek other scriptures.

. . . .

WHAT IS THIS WORK THAT Friedman has discovered—or, more precisely, restored—for us? It is the work known familiarly as J, generally recognized as the oldest authorial strand of the Pentateuch. But Friedman finds that J extends beyond the Pentateuch—into the biblical books of Joshua, Judges, Samuel, and Kings. Identifying the passages in these post-Pentateuchal books and attributing them to J is Friedman's contribution (#6).

• • • •

THIS IS THE DOCUMENTARY Hypothesis argument everyone should already know about. It comes from the 19th century when certain Bible scholars saw the different names for God and decided that different authors made their contribution to God's word.

• • • •

THE HYPOTHESIS IS ONLY founded on the names of God. There are no mentions anywhere in history, ancient documents, etc., of the existence of those works The same goes for Q for the NT. Plus, as usual, the proponents of this theory produce no physical evidence showing they have it right.

• • • •

IT IS JUST THEIR VIEW because they refuse to accept the fact that God uses many names, just as Jesus does. There was no late editor in the 5th to 7th centuries BC tying it all together into one big book.

• • • •

ACCORDING TO OUR MODERN understanding of this book, its oldest parts—such as the archaic tribal blessings in Genesis 49—were written in the premonarchic or early monarchic period of Israelite history (11th to 10th century B.C.E.). Its latest parts—including the last editorial touches by writers of the Priestly school—may come from the mid-fifth century B.C.E., the period of the priestly scribe Ezra,† who in Nehemiah chapter 8 reads "the Book of the Torah of Moses" to the people of Jerusalem for the first time, whereupon "all the people wept" (Nehemiah 8:9).† If this understanding is correct (and there are good reasons to think it is), then Genesis is a vast symphony in writing that took around five hundred years to complete (#7).

• • • •

WE ARE NOT GOING TO spend much time here as this is similar to the Documentary Hypothesis and removes Moses from authorship even though the author does not provide any real evidence supporting his view.

• • • •

IT IS HIS PERSONAL bias that he comes to this conclusion and nothing in the or about the Bible that leads him to that conclusion. It also comes from misreading the biblical texts and making giant leaps to conclusions. For example when the Bible says, something like 'are not the deeds of _____ written in the book of ____' the scholars leap to the assumption that that book was the source for the biblical author.

• • • •

THE AUTHOR IS MERELY sending people to a book where more details were recorded and not saying that is where he got his information.

• • • •

THE ANCIENT ISRAELITES were not a people of the book. King David had no Bible. Neither did the prophets. The later tradition that Moses wrote the Bible is never even mentioned in the biblical text. In biblical Israel animal sacrifice—not scripture—was the basis of worship. So how did the concept of a sacred written text develop? (#8).

• • • •

THIS IS AN AMAZING theory as it implies that scriptures basically appeared magically and that the Hebrews had nothing guiding their worship, telling them that they were doing it correctly or not.

• • • •

WHILE THERE WAS NO complete copy of the Hebrew Bible at that time, David was still writing his Psalms and Solomon had not written his books yet, and the same for some of the prophets, they still had the ark and Moses's book of the law inside the ark (Deut. 31: 25 to 26).

• • • •

IN OTHER WORDS, THEY still had scriptures to guide them. The people were not void of God's direction and they were not left to make their way to God on their own. The argument that it is not mentioned in the Bible that Moses wrote the Bible is a weak one as Moses did not write the whole Bible. He wrote the first 5 books.

• • • •

SO, THE SCHOLAR IS off base in her argument. God also had prophets to send his word to his people, the Hebrews were never void of any scripture at any time. The next quote tells you where this scholar feels who wrote the Bible.

• • • •

THE BIBLE ITSELF SUGGESTS that God's word—still mediated through the prophets—came to be understood as a written document only later, in the context of war and exile. Many scholars believe that the shock of the Babylonian destruction of Jerusalem in 586 B.C.E. and the subsequent Exile, with its threat of cultural oblivion through assimilation, prompted the conscious collection and written preservation of Israel's religious and historical traditions—a collection that eventually became our Bible (#9).

. . . .

IN HER MIND THERE WAS no single contributor but a collection of people trying desperately to hang onto their cultural identity. But again, if those scriptures were not true, when the exiles were returned to Israel the people there would know that those words were false and would refuse to accept them as scripture.

. . . .

THE TRUTH WOULD HAVE been passed down from father to son, mother to daughter as God commanded parents and grandparents to teach their children His commands and statuettes and any comparison would have exposed the fake texts (Deut. 4:9) and since the Hebrews had those scriptures long before their Exile, any fake writing would not be tolerated.

. . . .

FRIEDMAN ALSO EXPLORES the possibility that J might be a woman. He originally raised this issue in an earlier book, Who Wrote the Bible? (Engelwood Cliffs, NJ: Prentice Hall, 1987). Although the world of J is clearly a man's world, it nevertheless depicts numerous women who achieve very considerable power. Without acknowledging Friedman or his priority to this idea, Harold Bloom, in his best-selling book The Book of J (New York: Grove-Weidenfeld, 1990), picked up Friedman's suggestion and "transformed it into a full-blown claim (#10).

. . . .

THIS IS THE FINAL ARGUMENT that will be looked at in this section. Scholars tend to read into scriptures a lot. They think that modern values apply to ancient civilizations and to God's people and kingdom.

• • • •

THAT IS NOT THE CASE. The presence of 'powerful' women is not indication nor evidence that a woman wrote sections of the Bible. While there are two books named after women, Ruth and Esther, there is no evidence suggesting that women had a hand in their creation. It is a possibility, but we do not have anything concrete to form an opinion upon.

• • • •

THOSE BOOKS WERE ABOUT 2 women who played a very large role in Hebrew history. Their inclusion in the Bible shows that women can play a role in God's kingdom and Christianity. Women do not need to be named authors to be in that role.

• • • •

SOME POINTS TO CONSIDER

• • • •

KEEP IN MIND THAT OF all the arguments presented in the above section, not one of the scholars presented any real evidence that proves their point of view correct and the traditional view wrong.

• • • •

WHAT SETS THESE SCHOLARS off on their wild goose chases may be summed in the following quote:

• • • •

SINCE THE ENLIGHTENMENT, doubt about Mosaic authorship of the Pentateuch has characterized much biblical scholarship. Many small details in the text of the Pentateuch suggest that Moses himself could not have written all of it (e.g., the account of his death in Deut 34:1–12 or the account of his humility in Num 12:3). The evidence that Moses did not write everything, however, was taken instead as evidence that Moses must not have written anything (#11).

. . . . .

ONCE YOU OPEN THE DOOR, unbelievers and unbelieving scholars will walk in and take a mile for the inch that is given. They will use anything to support their unbelief and discredit God and his word. It is the same technique used by scholars who claim that the NT authors did not write their epistles.

. . . . .

FURTHER RESEARCH ON the Pentateuch has acknowledged the reality that language and style are not as useful for isolating sources as previously thought because individual words and phrases cannot be assigned to a single source in all cases without exception (#12).

. . . . .

THOSE SCHOLARS WILL use literary form, words, and other technical aspects of each book to determine who wrote what and then claim that the Bible is full of lies. God does not lie but unbelieving scholars can, and they lie about their technique being capable of discovering who really wrote which biblical book.

. . . . .

IT CAN'T AND THE SCHOLARS are just grasping at straws because they want the Bible to be like all the false religions scriptures-fake. That declaration enables them to live as they please, do as they want and say what they want. They get to be gods and create their own sense of morality and guidelines to live by instead of humbling themselves and accepting God's instructions.

• • • •

IT IS A STRANGE FACT that we biblical scholars always seem to meet people who are surprised that we really know things about the Bible (#13).

• • • •

SCHOLARS MAY KNOW SOME things about the Bible but there is a lot they do not know. If you remember the words of Dr. Stockton who said they do not know a lot about the Bible, then one of the two are misrepresenting what scholars know.

• • • •

ACTUALLY, SCHOLARS do not know who wrote the books of the Bible if they leave the traditional view. There are no ancient manuscripts giving them alternative information that can be verified.

• • • •

SCHOLARS ARE INFLUENCED by what they do or do not believe and cannot be objective in this matter. Nor can they uncover the truth as they are not following the Spirit of Truth, for the most part. There are some scholars who do but they deserve their own article showcasing their words.

• • • •

WHO WROTE THE BIBLE

• • • •

WHILE IT IS TRUE THAT we do not know the identity of every author for every book of the Bible, that does not mean those identities we do know are fakes, lies or frauds. The ancient church and the ancient Jewish people knew who wrote the books and their words must be taken seriously.

· · · · ·

THEY WOULD KNOW MORE about the authorship of the Bible than scholars who are 2,000 to 3,500 years removed from the fact. They also had more information as so many books have been lost over time depriving modern scholars of information they need to make any real conclusions on authorship.

· · · · ·

THE MEN WHO WROTE THE Bible had no special advantages. They had, most of them, little leisure, few books, and no learning, such as learning is reckoned in this world. Yet the book they compose is one which is unrivalled! There is but one way of accounting for this. They wrote under the direct inspiration of God (#14).

· · · · ·

WHILE WE CANNOT BE sure about the books and learning they had, some had elite training and others had Christ teaching them, they were inspired men and they were men who followed God's instructions in how to write his word.

· · · · ·

IT PROVES NOTHING, against inspiration, as some have asserted, that the writers of the Bible have each a different style. Isaiah does not write like Jeremiah, and Paul does not write like John. This is perfectly true—and yet the works of these men are not a whit less equally inspired (#15).

• • • •

THIS IS TRUE AND IT is a fact that trips up so many modern scholars. Even the authors of multiple books did not write in the same style as the issues were different, the people's spiritual maturity were and are different and so on.

• • • •

THEIR DIFFERENT STYLES do not mean that different authors wrote different books then lied about their identity. What it all boils down to is this, these men were inspired by God and they wrote what he wanted them to write.

• • • •

SO, THE TRUTH IS, GOD wrote the Bible and no one else. What anonymity of the human authors does is keep people's eyes on God and take them off the human vessel and the idea that the Bible is a human work.

• • • •

WHY DID GOD WRITE THE Bible

• • • •

THE ANSWER IS SIMPLE. He wanted to communicate to his creation the right way to live. He gives us instructions on how to please him, what is right, wrong, moral, immoral, good, and evil.

• • • •

WITHOUT THOSE WORDS we would be lost, and everyone would do what is right in their own eyes (Judges 17:6, 21:25). When people become believers, they are leaving one culture, the secular one and entering a new one- God's holy culture.

• • • •

THOSE CONVERTS NEED to know how to live in God's culture for it is vastly different than the one they are accustomed to. The Bible tells people how to live in God's culture.

• • • •

UNFORTUNATELY, THERE are too many people claiming to be Christians who cannot accept that concept or are misled to think that their preferences can be read into scripture. They confuse too many people and lead so many good believers astray.

• • • •

THAT IS WHY JESUS SAID he would send the spirit of truth to guide us. He knows the way to the truth and can help us identify it so all believers will be as the church in Acts was—of one mind and one faith.

• • • •

WE WILL RECOGNIZE THE truth because Jesus told us we would. We just have to have faith in him. It is God's kingdom we are entering thus we need the Bible to know God's rules in order to live in his kingdom.

• • • •

WE ALSO NEED TO KNOW the real author for that tells us the Bible is credible and the rules are real. God did not leave us without instruction or guidance. We are a light unto this world because we live according to the rules of God's kingdom.

• • • •

WORKS CITED:

• • • •

#1. BARUCH HALPERN VIA the Naked Archaeologist television show episode Who Wrote the Bible https://www.youtube.com/watch?v=SyTkHbyRcko (2005)

#2. Stockton, R., (2018), "Who Wrote The Bible? This Is What The Actual Historical Evidence Says", ATI, retrieved from https://allthatsinteresting.com/who-wrote-the-bible

#3. Ibid

#4. Ehrman, BD, (2011), "Who Wrote The Bible and Why It Matters", Huffpost, retrieved from https://www.huffpost.com/entry/the-bible-telling-lies-to_b_840301

#5. Propp, W., (2006), "Exorcising Demons", Bible Review, 20(5).

#6. Shanks, H., (2004), "Has Richard Friedman Really Discovered a Long-Hidden Book in the Bible? Friedman's Thesis: An Overview", Bible Review, 15(2)

#7. Hendel, RS, (2005), "Genesis and the Cathedrals: Like a French cathedral, Genesis was built over time", Bible Review, 21(5)

#8. Winn Leith, MJ., (2004), "From Storm to Scroll: How the thundering voice of God became sacred scripture", Bible Review, 18(4).

#9. Ibid

#10 Op Cit Shanks (2004)

#11 Mangum, D., Custis, M., & Widder, W. (2012). Genesis 1–11, Lexham Commentary, Bellingham, WA: Lexham Press.

#12 Ibid

#13 Friedman, RE, (2004), "Is Everybody a Bible Expert?: Not the authors of the Book of J", Bible Review, 7(2)

#14 Ryle, J. C. (1853), "How Readest Thou?", Startling Questions (p. 155). New York: Robert Carter & Brothers.

#15. Ibid

Dealing With the Minimalists

IN ARCHAEOLOGY

. . . .

THERE ARE GENERALLY two schools of thought. The Maximalists school supports the biblical record and sees it as very historical. The other school of thought is the Minimalist. This group takes the opposing side of the argument and dismiss much of the biblical record as fake news, to cite a modern term.

. . . .

IF BIBLICAL ARCHAEOLOGY is to have a future, then those participating in the field must learn the Minimalists' arguments and look to God to help them find the right information to refute the Minimalists' claims.

. . . .

IT IS IMPERATIVE THAT the biblical archaeologist does this as they are the ones qualified to handle the task. Like the Minimalist scholar or archaeologist, the biblical archaeologist has the schooling, the experience and have studied the same discoveries.

. . . .

THIS IS NOT A TASK that can be left up to the ordinary believer. The majority of believers would be in over their heads and it would take years for them to get up to speed before they could handle the job.

. . . .

THERE IS A CERTAIN urgency to completing this task as the regular church goer actually comes face to face with a similar group of people in their daily lives and at their places of employment.

• • • •

WHILE YOU READ THIS chapter, you should come to the realization that the professional archaeologist and bible scholar who takes the minimalist view are nothing more than normal unbelievers.

• • • •

THEY ARE A GROUP OF people who do archaeology and study the Bible yet refuse to or are unable to take that leap of faith and accept God's word. Their education levels, their experience levels, or their knowledge of a vast number of languages should not intimidate the biblical archaeologist or the common believer.

• • • •

THESE MEN AND WOMEN have made a decision to reject what God has said and they do not have the spirit of truth helping them thus their views are not from God and are generally wrong.

• • • •

THIS CHAPTER EXPLORES the topic of Minimalists. Even though a regular church member does not come in contact with this group of people, that they know of, in reality the regular church goer runs into the same type of people all the time. An unbeliever is an unbeliever no matter how well educated they are or how great is their class standing.

• • • •

THE DEFINITION OF A Minimalist

. . . .

IT IS NOT HARD TO FIND a definition of the term Minimalist. In non-archaeological life the first part of the word 'minimal' indicates that the person is not going to accept a large portion of information presented to them. Dr. Paul Maier describes then in this fashion:

. . . .

A GROUP OFTEN STYLED as "Biblical minimalists" sees little or no correlation between archaeological and Biblical evidence, and thus no reliable history in the Hebrew Bible (the Old Testament). Leading spokesmen among the minimalists are Thomas L. Thompson and Niels P. Lemche of the University of Copenhagen, with like-minded, postmodernist colleagues in both hemispheres (#1).

. . . .

WHAT THE MINIMALIST does is reject much of the archaeological evidence that is uncovered showing that the historical portions of the Bible are true and can be verified. Even Joseph's slave price as verified by Kenneth Kitchen is rejected as Joseph is not mentioned in any extra biblical texts (#2).

. . . .

THIS THOUGHT IS BACKED up by the following words:

. . . .

THAT THESE BIBLICAL figures have not shown up in extra-Biblical records is part of Sperling's demonstration that the Biblical accounts are "unhistorical (#3).

. . . .

THOSE QUOTED WORDS provide an excellent definition for the term Minimalist. They are a group of people who reject biblical history simply because there are not extra biblical texts supporting the accounts of the Bible.

. . . .

THIS PUTS THE BIBLICAL accounts into a very one-sided argument with the Minimalist supposedly holding all the cards. Without extra biblical inclusion, they simply shake their heads and say the biblical account did not happen.

. . . .

THIS DENIAL IS DONE with the Minimalist knowing full well of the limitations of archaeology and the destruction that takes place over time. In other words, the biblical accounts do not stand a chance with these types of people because they think they get to set the standards for what did or did not take place in history.

. . . .

THE ARGUMENTS OF THE Minimalists

. . . .

ONE OF THE THINGS YOU will notice in the Minimalist arguments is that their denials come from silence. They never produce any real physical evidence to support their case, whether biblical or extra biblical. They actually violate their own rules as they accept and believe their versions without any direct evidence providing confirmation to those views.

. . . .

THE READER SHOULD BE aware that we have no direct evidence of the existence of characters best known to readers of the Bible, including—but not limited to—Abraham, Sarah, Isaac, Jacob, Esau, Moses, Joshua, Deborah, Gideon, David, Goliath, and Solomon." So writes Rabbi S. David Sperling, professor of Bible and chair of the faculty at Hebrew Union College—Jewish Institute of Religion in New York, in his recent book The Original Torah.† Sperling contends that the Pentateuch is, to use his term, "unhistorical." ... Therefore, he concludes, "I am compelled to read the Torah allegorically because it cannot be read historically" (#4).

. . . .

THIS IS JUST ONE OF the arguments the Minimalists present to the biblical archaeologist and general believer. Rabbi Sperling uses the term direct evidence which is his way of ignoring all the indirect evidence, see Kitchen's work above, that has shown the Bible to be accurate in what it talks about. They will not accept God's word on the topic even though God is the only eyewitness left alive today and knows what actually took place.

. . . .

GOD AS AN EYEWITNESS is not subject to the factors many legal analysts claim ruin the eyewitness testimony of people seeing a crime. He is not going to fabricate tales and then turn around and say that his followers cannot lie. That would make God a hypocrite and he would be sinning, disqualifying him from his claim to being God.

. . . .

THAT RABBI HOLDS THAT opinion even though direct evidence for another figure in the Old Testament has been found:

. . . .

WE KNOW FROM THE BIBLE about an Ammonite king named Ba'alis who lived in the sixth century B.C. If we were writing a few years ago we could correctly state that there was no extra-Biblical reference to Ba'alis—even a king went unmentioned. Now he has turned up twice in the extra-Biblical record. There are numerous instances like this (#5).

• • • •

ANOTHER ARGUMENT THE Minimalist uses is that the Bible was edited and not write at the time it was describing.

• • • •

WHAT ABOUT THE BIBLICAL minimalists, people such as Thomas Thompson and Niels Peter Lemche of the University of Copenhagen and Philip Davies and Keith Whitelam of the University of Sheffield, who say the Bible has no value for historical purposes, at least for the history of the period being described? Perhaps, they say, the Biblical text can tell us something about the period when it was written, but not about the period it chronicles, which the minimalists claim was hundreds of years earlier (#6).

• • • •

IN OTHER WORDS, THE minimalist decides that the Bible could not have been written at the time for whatever reason they may use. Only later generations were capable of putting the text on paper and the preceding hundreds of years, those accounts were transmitted orally and horribly distorted.

• • • •

AGAIN, THOUGH, THIS argument is from silence as there is no direct physical evidence proving that accusation true. Nor is there any manuscript evidence pointing the fact that the Old Testament historical sections were penned centuries after they took place.

. . . .

ORIGINAL COPIES OF the Old Testament have been lost for thousands of years. A third argument that the Minimalist falls back on is the accusation that the Old Testament history was written for political reasons:

. . . .

BY THIS HE MEANS THAT the text can tell us nothing about the period of which it speaks, only about the time hundreds of years later when the text was composed—and the stories made up. The stories in the Torah, he contends, are "politically charged texts [that] provide historical evidence [only] for the period in which they were composed." (#7).

. . . .

UNFORTUNATELY FOR THE Minimalist, if that were true, the Old Testament would not have made it out of the 5th or 6th Centuries BC. There would be more than enough people who would know the actual truth and not accept those historical books as scriptures.

. . . .

THE POLITICAL ANGLE would fall apart as soon as a new set of governing officials replaced the old ones. The new officials could easily rewrite the texts to fit their points of view, telling the people that the previous versions were full of errors. There are no manuscripts depicting this change thus the Old Testament historical books are accurate accounts of what took place in Israel's history.

. . . .

THEN THE PEOPLE OF Israel would have their own historical records they could check to see if they were being told the truth or not. Once it was discovered they weren't, there is nothing stopping the people from demanding a rewrite, so the truth is included in their holy book.

• • • •

NEXT THE MINIMALIST creates their own history and states that the biblical Israel was not the real Israel and their history is now lost.

• • • •

IN SHORT, CRITICAL Biblical scholars now realize that the two Israels—the Biblical Israel and the historical Israel—should not, indeed cannot, be brought together. The problem is not a scientific one, but a theological and political one for those who think the Bible has to be history if it is not to be worthless. Unfortunately, Biblical scholars are in a discipline where scientific views are most under pressure from those who think that religious and political arguments have some weight (#8).

• • • •

THE SAME REBUTTALS that take down the other arguments also work against this one. There is also nothing stopping any 'real Israelite' from recording the actual history of his people and hiding it away till a better time arose where it could be presented.

• • • •

PLUS, IF THE BIBLICAL authors got it wrong, there is nothing stopping God from raising up someone to rewrite the history and get the truth to the people. Science is not the issue here as it has no authority over what was done in the past. Common sense rules in this instance and it does not make sense for anyone to fabricate his nation's history.

. . . .

ONCE IT WAS FOUND OUT the history was fabricated, he or his family would suffer greatly by the anger of the people. These are just some of the main arguments used by the Minimalist to ignore the biblical record.

. . . .

THE POINTS OF THE MINIMALIST

. . . .

THE SCHOOL OF THOUGHT called the Minimalist have constructed some fundamental points they feel pertain to the Israel of history. These points out line their position quite well yet again, they offer no real direct physical evidence other than silence.

. . . .

THE HEBREW BIBLE IS a product of the religious and cultural "identity crisis" of Judaism in the Hellenistic era, not the story of an actual historical Israel in the long-gone Iron Age.

. . . .

-THE HEBREW BIBLE THUS constitutes a literary tradition, not a historical document; it is a "social construct" that reflects the religious interests and propaganda of a late, elitist theocratic party within Judaism. It reveals their history, if any.

-It follows that "Biblical" and "ancient" Israel are fictitious myths invented by the Biblical writers, not historical realities. Even if a "historical Israel" in the Iron Age could be reconstructed, it would consist of a very brief outline of a handful of later kings and a few skeletal political events, corroborated mainly by extra-Biblical texts.

-There was no "early Israel" as a distinct ethnic entity in the Iron I period in Palestine, no Israelite state before the ninth century B.C.E., no Judahite state before the late eighth century B.C.E., no significant political capital in Jerusalem before the second century B.C.E.

-Archaeologists and Biblical scholars should now concentrate on writing the history of the Palestinian peoples, not that of some imaginary "ancient Israel." (#9).

• • • •

WHAT THESE POINTS ARE saying is that the Minimalist does not and refuses to believe God. They do not accept God's word and will not use faith that God is not lying to them. Instead, they have set themselves up as judges of God and his writers even though they have no authority to make that promotion.

• • • •

ALSO, WITH NO DIRECT evidence for an actual Israel that was a nation that was fundamentally different from the biblical one, the Minimalist is creating the exact same fantasy they accuse the biblical authors of creating.

• • • •

THERE IS NO EXTRA BIBLICAL evidence supporting their alternative country thus their own arguments must be used to reject their alternative ideas. Until the Minimalist turns up such extra biblical evidence, their arguments are moot.

• • • •

THE ERRORS ARE NOT there

• • • •

THE BIBLICAL TEXT IS not a human written book. If it were it may have been possible for it to be subject to editing in later centuries. But this is not the case. The words of the biblical authors are not the words of someone writing long after the fact. As Dr. Halpern points out:

· · · ·

IF THE BOOKS OF KINGS were wholly, or even largely, a product of the Persian era and written without access to pre-exilic sources (as the "minimalists" claim with regard to the United Monarchy of David and Solomon), we should expect multiple errors both in chronology and in the names of major public figures, such as kings. Herodotus, writing at the very time Davies, Thompson and Van Seters posit the activity of our biblical authors, commits such errors with obstinate regularity, despite the fact that he traveled extensively in the lands on which he reports. He relied, it would seem, primarily on oral sources (#10).

· · · ·

WHAT HE IS SAYING IS that the biblical authors, much to the disappointment of the Minimalist, did not commit the errors one would expect to see if they were writing long after the fact and relying on oral sources.

· · · ·

THE BIBLICAL AUTHORS got everything right which is direct evidence pointing to the fact that they were writing at the time the events took place. The facts show that the Minimalist arguments are missing the right type of evidence and rely on nothing but the personal opinion and preference of the Minimalist.

· · · ·

CONCLUSION

• • • •

THE CHALLENGE THAT Biblical scholarship faces today is to explain that the Bible is not history, or at least cannot be used as a blueprint for a history—and also that this unavoidable conclusion does not devalue the Bible (#11).

• • • •

NO, THE CHALLENGE IS on the Minimalist for they are making extraordinary claims about the Bible. It is not up to the Biblical Archaeologist to run around digging up half the Holy Land or the Sinai Peninsula just to find evidence that would please the Minimalist.

• • • •

GOD HAS SET THE RULES and it is not up to the Biblical Archaeologist to ignore those rules. They do not waste their time trying to please unbelieving men and women. Instead, they need to gently remind the Minimalist and other unbelievers that God has set the rule that faith is involved.

• • • •

THAT MEANS THAT NO matter how hard anyone digs in the sand, there is not going to be so much physical evidence that will undermine that rule. The Biblical Archaeologist can continue digging looking for the truth while learning to use the evidence to identify the Minimalist's arguments and refute them through logical and rational means.

• • • •

IT IS NOT UP TO BIBLICAL scholarship to give the Minimalist what they want. It is up to biblical scholarship to find the truth and publish that. With the Minimalist arguments there is no real starting point as they do not have a shorter timeline than 3 centuries where the supposed editing took place.

• • • •

THEY ALSO DO NOT HAVE the names of those editors, extra biblical resources that describe those activities taking place and so on. The challenge then is on the Minimalist to produce those pieces of evidence for objective study before any changes to the nature of the Bible can take place.

• • • •

SO FAR, NO MINIMALIST has produced one shred of credible and verifiable physical, direct or indirect, evidence proving they are on the right track. The Minimalist takes the easy route and just deny, deny, and deny. There is no work involved when all one has to do is deny the truth.

• • • •

AS IT STANDS, THERE has not been one manuscript discovery that shows that the Old Testament was altered in any way. The Bible stands as written to be true. There is no argument that will change that fact.

• • • •

WORKS CITED

• • • •

#1. MAIER, P. L. (2004). Archaeology—Biblical Ally or Adversary? Bible and Spade, 17(3), 82.

#2. Longman III, T, (2019), "The Joseph Story", Bible odyssey, retrieved from https://www.bibleodyssey.org/en/tools/video-gallery/j/joseph-story

#3. Shanks, H., (1999), "First Person: The Meaning of Unhistory", BAR, 25(3).

#4. Ibid

#5. Ibid

#6. Shanks, H., (2000), "The Age of BAR: Scholars Talk About How the Field Has Changed, BAR, 27(2).

#7. Op Cit Shanks (1999)

#8. Davies, PR., (2000), "The Search for History in the Bible: What Separates a Minimalist from a Maximalist? Not Much", BAR, 26(2).

#9. Dever, WG, (2000), "The Search for History in the Bible: Save Us from Postmodern Malarkey", BAR, 26(2).

#10 Halpern, B., (2004), "Erasing History: The minimalist assault on ancient Israel", Bible Review, 11(6).

#11. Op cit Davies (2000)

The Problem of Illiteracy

INTRODUCTION

. . . . .

IF BIBLICAL ARCHAEOLOGY is to have a future it must not buy into the many tales that archaeologists and scholars' tale. One of those tales is that the ancient world was illiterate. What fuels this story in part is how modern archaeologists view the research field of Archaeology.

. . . . .

ACCORDING TO DR. W.M. Dever, archaeology remains an unedited field of research until it hits the hands of the professional archaeologist's hands. (#1). This is a very revealing concept as it shows how unrealistic professional archaeologists, including biblical ones, really are.

. . . . .

THIS CONCEPT DOES NOT allow room for the limitations of the field to play any influential role. Under this thinking, it is assumed that biblical archaeologists are finding virgin discoveries that have lain untouched for centuries.

. . . . .

THAT THINKING ALSO ignores that time, natural and other calamities have played roles in the positioning of the remains and what items are extant and which ones are never seen. These limitations of archaeology play a very key role in what is found in relation to issues like literacy.

. . . .

ANOTHER REVEALING FACTOR found in that statement is that those archaeologists who agree with Dr. Dever's sentiments is that many biblical and other archaeologists feel that the elites of the ancient world played more of a role than they actually may have done.

. . . .

WHAT FURTHER COMPOUNDS this issue is the mis-identification of ancient buildings that eliminate the possibility that the ancient cities actually had schools where their children went to be educated.

. . . .

YET, EVEN WITH CHANGES to the attitude about the past and to the identification of larger buildings, knowing about the literacy of the ancient world remains a subjective topic.

. . . .

GIVEN THE AMOUNT OF the inscriptions, texts, laws, and other written material that survives from the past, the question must be asked, who were the authors writing to if the majority of the ancient world was illiterate? (This question is not original with the author. The original person asking the question has been lost over time).

Was the ancient world illiterate

. . . .

THE ANSWER TO THIS question depends on whom you are talking to. In his lecture series, he placed the literacy rate for the ancient Hebrew people at 1 to 2% (#2). That is a very low figure and one that he presents no documentation to support his estimate.

• • • •

THAT SEEMS TO BE A very conservative figure given that most archaeological sites have 98 to 95% of their area and contents undiscovered. Whether those contents and buildings, etc. Were destroyed through natural elements, wars, or just time itself is not the point. It is hard to accept such a low figure when most of the information about the local people is lost (#3).

• • • •

BUT DR. DEVER IS NOT alone in his assessment of the lack of literacy in ancient Israel. A recent discovery of some soldiers writing 16 inscriptions or documents at a military base have suffered a similar fate:

• • • •

NOW OUR JOB IS TO EXTRAPOLATE from Arad to a broader area," said Prof. Finkelstein. "Adding what we know about Arad to other forts and administrative localities across ancient Judah, we can estimate that many people could read and write during the last phase of the First Temple period. We assume that in a kingdom of some 100,000 people, at least several hundred were literate."(#4).

• • • •

THAT CONCLUSION BY Dr. Israel Finkelstein is not very flattering to the Hebrew military personal nor to the people in general. It also doesn't say much for those who were literate, if his numbers are correct. He is basically stating that those who were literate had no desire to teach anyone else and left the illiterate to their fate.

• • • •

IT ISN'T JUST ANCIENT Israel that is being condemned by modern scholars and archaeologists. Other ancient nations like Egypt,

Rome and even Greece are all placed under the same label regardless of extraneous facts and mitigating factors.

• • • •

THESE SCHOLARS COME up with a bunch of different excuses in order to justify their conclusion that the ancient world was unintelligent and incapable of learning their ABCs:

• • • •

MOST PEOPLE IN ANCIENT Egypt did not know how to read and write. Since the majority of Egyptians were peasant farmers, they would not have needed to learn to read, and the complexities of the written language would have made it more difficult to learn than most alphabetic writing systems (#5).

• • • •

THE LANGUAGE THAT THEY spoke was too difficult for them to learn how to read or write? That is a bit off the wall since growing up with the language and using it every day is a sure-fire way to learn how to read and write it. Farmers need to be literate just like everyone else does.

• • • •

THEY HAVE BUSINESS concerns and they need to keep track of their income, expenditures and write bill of sales and so on. Just because they were farmers does not mean they refused or could not have the intelligence to learn to read or write.

• • • •

THE CONCLUSION OF THAT author shows that he does not consider the idea that the children of those farmers were discontented with farm life and sought to expand their horizons which would necessitate learning how to read and write.

• • • •

WHEN ROMAN LITERATURE finally emerged, it developed not from native roots but out of the Greek literary tradition. Greek literature spread to Rome during the Hellenistic* period. The first appearance of literature in the Latin language is a translation from the 200s B.C. of Homer's Greek epic the Odyssey. The first Roman writers translated, adapted, and imitated the works of Homer and other Greek masters. Having absorbed Greek literary forms, Roman literature suddenly flourished, and writing became a fundamental part of Roman culture (#6).

• • • •

THAT IS A NICE GUESS but in order to be able to copy those works one must know their own language quite well. Plus, that native language must have been in use for some time in order to properly make translations.

• • • •

LATIN MAY HAVE MADE its first appearance in the 200 BC era but that does not mean the language did not exist prior to that time. All it means is that any previous works have been lost due to a variety of issues. That excuse is outlandish at best and ignores the reality of life in any society.

• • • •

ONE CANNOT JUDGE THE literacy of any nation based on the lack of physical evidence. Then the author above literally contradicts himself with the following words:

• • • •

LITTLE WRITING HAS survived from the earliest period of Roman culture except for some laws and religious inscriptions. During the early republic, the Romans inscribed documents on tablets for public view, as the Greeks had done. These include the famous Twelve Tables, the first Roman law code, which was displayed in the Roman Forum. However, the Romans during this period wrote no literature that has survived to the present (#7).

• • • •

THE QUESTION THAT NEEDS to be asked is, if the early Romans were illiterate, why would they need to post laws, etc., for public viewing? If the common people could not read nor write then that would be a wasted effort as literary people, if small in number, would not be around those postings 24 hours a day 7 days a week to help their fellow citizens to read the texts.

• • • •

THE ARGUMENTS AGAINST a literate ancient world make no sense and rely more on silence than on anything else. To illustrate this point just look at the United States of America. 350,000,000 people strong, and not every person leaves writing behind or if they did, tornadoes, fires, theft and other calamities would have destroyed what they did record.

• • • •

THAT 350 MILLION FIGURE is the approx. population of the nation today. What about the hundreds of millions that came before? Under the arguments listed above, future archaeologists may hold that nation illiterate because English is one of the toughest languages to learn, people did not leave lots of handwriting samples around and even the military men and women do not do a lot of writing.

. . . .

YET WE KNOW THAT AMERICA has a strong educational system and almost all of its people get a chance to learn to read and write. The few that do not and are illiterate are not testimony that the rest of the population could not read nor write.

. . . .

ALSO, THE FACT THAT everyone does not leave written records does not mean they were not educated in the public school system, whose lessons include learning how to read and write.

. . . .

SOME ISSUES SURROUNDING the debate

. . . .

IT IS UNDERSTANDABLE why certain archaeologists and biblical scholars leap to the conclusion that the ancient world was illiterate. Physical evidence has a hard time surviving when it is placed in the wrong environment.

. . . .

PAPYRUS AND LEATHER documents have not survived from most of Palestine, only from very arid regions such as the area around the Dead Sea. These materials rot in damp soil. The fact that they have not been discovered does not mean, therefore, that they did not exist (#8).

. . . .

THIS PRESENTS A PROBLEM to the modern-day scholar or biblical archaeologist. No one knows how much was lost because no one knows how much written material was actually recorded. Just because a few fragments survive does not mean that only the authors of those fragments could read or write. It just means that much of the information was lost due to time, destruction, and other factors.

• • • •

THE FAMOUS LIBRARY of Alexandria is a prime example of what may have been lost, even in ancient times. There is an estimate that somewhere between 700,000 and 1,000,000 scrolls were destroyed in that fire. How many authors lost their works is unknown, but the question remains who were these authors writing to? They certainly would not have made any money if they were only writing to the elites (#9).

• • • •

THAT FIGURE DOES NOT include all the people who may have learned to read and write yet never put pen to paper, so to speak, unless they were writing a note to their spouse, children or friends.

• • • •

HARRIS, KEITH, AND others, however, have challenged the notion of widespread literacy in the ancient world due to the lack of financial, political, social, and organizational capacity. Harris suggests that only 10 percent of the population, consisting primarily of male elites, would have been literate (#10).

• • • •

HOW CAN DR. HARRIS come up with such a figure? The extant data does not support such a low number nor provides enough information to warrant such an insult to the community and its leaders.

With hundreds of thousands of inscriptions, inscribed pottery sherds and ancient manuscripts stored in museums around the world, it is impossible to state that so few people knew how to read or write.

. . . .

THAT POINT IS SUPPORTED by the following words:

. . . .

IT IS DIFFICULT TO know how widespread the ability to read or write was in the ancient world. Neither the Greeks nor the Romans kept statistics on literacy rates as modern countries do. Scholars have estimated that at the high point of Greek civilization, fewer than one-third of the adult population could read or write. Even so, literacy was more widespread in the Greco-Roman world than it was in many other ancient civilizations, where the ability to read or write was limited to a small number of priests or scribes (#11).

. . . .

EVEN IF THEY DID KEEP those records, they have not been dug up yet, which further perpetuates the myth that the ancient world was illiterate. That final sentence has no physical evidence to support its claim.

. . . .

IT IS ASSUMED RATHER exegeted out of ancient records that the ancient people were illiterate. There is no reason to paint such a bleak picture as no archaeologist, biblical or otherwise, knows the truth on this issue. They just do not have the data to support their blind generality.

. . . .

FINALLY, ANCIENT RECORDS do hold some information to the fact that the ancient world was more literate than the modern archaeologist gives it credit for:

• • • •

THE FIRST-CENTURY A.D. Jewish historian Josephus reports that, when the First Jewish Revolt against Rome broke out in 66 A.D., one of the rebels' primary targets was an archive building in Jerusalem that housed debt records they wanted to burn.† They knew the power these records could have over them (#12).

• • • •

RECORDS WERE KEPT, where they were kept was well known and the meaning behind those records was quite well understood. It is far-fetched to assume that the ancient world was not literate.

• • • •

CONCLUSION

• • • •

WHILE IT IS A GIVEN that not every section of ancient society enjoyed literacy, just as the modern American one has, those who were illiterate do not speak for the condition of the rest of society.

• • • •

THERE MAY HAVE BEEN long periods where people were not educated properly but that does not mean every ancient civilization in every era was illiterate. The logistics alone testifies against such conclusions.

• • • •

THERE WOULD NOT BE enough elites or scribes to handle all the writing of inscriptions, etc., and why would they write them if they already understood the words? The public, according to some modern archaeologists, would not understand them, could not read them so why waste the effort and the expense to write things down or have them carved in stone?

• • • •

MANY MODERN ARCHAEOLOGISTS do not think these things through. They get what they want and then paint their picture of how they want the past to be. Once that is done, they rarely change their minds on the topic.

• • • •

IT IS HIGHLY DOUBTFUL that ancient governments would waste their money on a project that would be useless in the long run. All they had to do is send out a few town criers and the news, laws or other accomplishment would be known by the public at a cheaper cost.

• • • •

EGOS HAVE LITTLE TO do with it as how would a ruler's ego be fueled, if the people could not read what was written? The goal would be met through oral renditions that got the word out.

• • • •

THERE ARE JUST TOO many inscriptions, manuscripts and so on, created in the ancient world to justify the idea that the ancient world was illiterate. Deut. 6: 9 and Habakkuk 2:2 are just 2 verses that indicate that the common man knew how to read and write.

• • • •

THERE ARE 64 MORE VERSES that deal with reading and writing in the Bible. Even with the existence of oral tradition, reading and writing still can and does take place. The presence of oral traditions does not mean the people were illiterate.

• • • •

THE CONCLUSION TO THE opposite is based on nothing but personal preference and how the archaeologist wants the ancient world to be. It is an attitude the biblical archaeologist cannot afford to have.

• • • •

CLAIMING THAT THE ANCIENTS were illiterate is an insult to every ancient society and to God. That is standing in judgment of people most modern archaeologists know nothing about.

• • • •

WORKS CITED

• • • •

#1. DEVER, WM., (2009), "How Archaeology Illuminates the Bible, 8 Lectures for Biblical Archaeology Society on 2 CDs

#2. Ibid

#3. Kitchen, K., (2004), The Bible In Its World, chapter 1. Wipf & Stock Pub.

#4. Arutz Sheva Staff, (2016), "600 BCE inscriptions prove ancient Jewish literacy", retrieved from http://www.israelnationalnews.com/News/News.aspx/210694

#5. Farid, M., (2012), "Literacy in Ancient Egypt", Astromic Backyard, retrieved from https://astromic.blogspot.com/2012/09/literacy-in-ancient-egypt.html

#6. AHC, (2020), "Literacy", Home Ancient History & Civilisation Ancient Greece and Rome: An Encyclopedia for Students

(4 Volume Set) Page 257, retrieved from https://erenow.net/ancient/ancient-greece-and-rome-an-encyclopedia-for-students-4-volume-set/257.php

#7. Ibid

#8. Millard, A., (2003), "Literacy in the Time of Jesus: Could His words have been recorded in His lifetime?", BAR, 29(4).

#9. DHWTY, (2019), "Who Destroyed the Great Library of Alexandria?", Ancient Origins, retrieved from https://www.ancient-origins.net/ancient-places-africa-history-important-events/destruction-great-library-alexandria-001644

#10 Foster, C. G. (2016). Scribe, Critical Issues. In J. D. Barry, D. Bomar, D. R. Brown, R. Klippenstein, D. Mangum, C. Sinclair Wolcott, ... W. Widder (Eds.), The Lexham Bible Dictionary. Bellingham, WA: Lexham Press.

#11. Op Cit AHC (2020)

#12. Op Cit Millard, (2003

The Biblical Archaeologist & Carthage

WE MUST FOLLOW THE rules

• • • •

THIS WAS TOLD TO THIS author by Mr. Henry Smith of the Associates for Biblical research when the two had a discussion over his 2013 article on Carthage and Child Sacrifice. The rules that were being alluded to by Mr. Smith went something like the extant ancient authors must be believed even when there is no opposing content or supporting evidence for their words.

• • • •

THOSE RULES, IF THEY really do exist, were written by unbelieving scholars and archaeologists as far as this author can tell. If anyone actually follows those rules, then they are getting their research off on the wrong foot and blind themselves to the truth.

• • • •

THEIR WORK BECOMES distorted as does history and the truth is lost because the rules were written in favor of the prevailing acceptable archaeological position. This is distressing as biblical archaeologists have a mandate to search for and write the truth.

• • • •

JESUS SAID WE WOULD know the truth and following the wrong rules only interferes with that direction. It is not the purpose of this chapter to decide if the people of Carthage did or did not sacrifice their children to their gods.

• • • •

THESE WERE UNBELIEVING people and it is unrealistic to expect them to follow Christian rules or even OT rules when they did not adhere to those faiths. The possibility is always there but in analyzing the past, the Biblical archaeologist must remain open minded, honest as well as fair.

. . . . .

WHAT HAS BEEN PUBLISHED in scholarly works is far from those characteristics, even when the Biblical Archaeologist publishing those articles on Carthage are Christian. The point of this chapter is to point out the weaknesses of those published opinions and to strive to provide the Biblical archaeologist the correct way to look at the past.

. . . .

THE WE BELIEVE ARGUMENT

. . . .

MODERN SCHOLARS HAVE given the name Tophet to places where they believe child sacrifice took place around the Mediterranean rim, mostly famously at Carthage. We believe it is apparent that the Phoenicians brought this barbaric practice to Carthage from Canaan, and therefore, evidence of child sacrifice at Carthage provides support for the historicity of the biblical accounts (#1).

. . . .

THIS IS AN ARGUMENT used by secular scientists, scholars, experts, and even Christian ones. The person making the statements or writing the paper are only stating their opinion not presenting any facts.

. . . .

WHILE THIS MAY SEEM like a good way to get a point to the people it is erroneous because it is only a guess that is not supported in fact. While there is no doubt that the ancient people of Carthage may have brought their religious beliefs to their new city, the remaining records do show this, but those records do not support the idea that child sacrifice was practiced.

· · · ·

THE 'I BELIEVE' ARGUMENT also ignores facts allowing the speaker to cherry pick what ancient evidence they will accept and which ones they will reject. One of those facts is the loss of all official and public records.

· · · ·

EVENTUALLY IN 146 BC, as a result of a final war, Carthage was razed to the ground, and its North African kingdom was constituted a Roman province under the name of Africa. War with the Celts in North Italy, commencing the next year, resulted in the extension of the boundary to the Alps, and countries beyond began to feel the terror of the Roman name (#2).

· · · ·

WHEN FACED WITH THIS reality, people are free to believe what they want as there is no real evidence to contradict the 'I believe' argument. The person using the I believe argument is free to read into the evidence whatever they like it to say.

· · · ·

THERE IS NO NEED TO be objective or honest as those using this method of describing the past are working from silence and possibly one-sided ancient information, which in Carthage's case is true.

• • • •

MR. VINE'S WORDS IN that quote are supported by the main archaeologists who the majority of modern scholars cite when they write or talk about this topic. Their words are as follows:

• • • •

INDEED, SOIL IN THE Carthage Tophet was found to be full of olive wood charcoal, no doubt from the sacrificial pyres. We have no idea how the Phoenicians themselves referred to the places of burning or burial or to the practice itself, since no large body of Phoenician writing—no Phoenician "Bible," as it were—has come down to us (#3).

• • • •

NOTICE THAT THERE IS nothing available for the archaeologist to use to form their opinion. The Romans did a great job in destroying all the official records, laws and other manuscripts which could have shed light on this issue.

• • • •

WHEN THIS SITUATION arises, the biblical archaeologist needs to take a step back and stop themselves from condemning an ancient people because as it stands, archaeology is blind to the past when all it has are stone artifacts lacking in data to look at and 'interpret'.

• • • •

THE ENEMY'S WORD IS not good enough

• • • •

THIS IS ONE OF THE vital portions in the debate about if child sacrifice took place or not. All modern scholars have are the words of a few ancient writers who did not go into much detail but made sweeping generalizations and accusations against the people of Carthage. It should be pointed out that these ancient writers were the enemy of Carthage.

. . . .

EVIDENCE FROM CLASSICAL authors. Ancient authors, both Greco-Roman historians like Kleitarchos, Diodorus and Plutarch and Church fathers like Tertullian, condemn the Carthaginians for the practice of child sacrifice. Some add lurid but unverifiable details—sacrifices witnessed by distraught mothers, grimacing victims consumed by flames, human offerings received in the outstretched arms of a brazen statue. On one point these sources are completely in accord: The Carthaginians sacrificed their children to their supreme deities (#4).

. . . .

WHILE THESE ANCIENT authors' words must be considered it cannot be considered without using the influence of scriptures to honestly look at what these men were writing.

. . . .

FIRST OFF, THESE ANCIENT writers, save for Tertullian, were no believers and were not following God's rules on how to write about others. They have no real objective moral standard imposed by a Supreme Being to guide their words.

. . . .

THAT MEANS THAT THEY were free to write whatever they wanted about the people of Carthage. With so few ancient documents making it intact to the modern world, there is no way to verify their words as true.

• • • •

THAT IS ESPECIALLY so when other extant ancient authors writing on the same people do not mention child sacrifice.

• • • •

TO BE SURE, SOME HISTORIANS who wrote about Carthage, such as Polybius, took no note of this practice. Why Polybius failed to mention Carthaginian child sacrifice is a mystery. He was a member of Scipio's staff in 146 B.C., and he must have known the city well (#5).

• • • •

AS EVERYONE ALREADY knows there are many reasons why Polybius failed to mention child sacrifice. One of those reasons may have been that child sacrifice was not practiced by all the citizens; if it were practiced by a few, that may have been done in private so no one would know and so on.

• • • •

THE PROBLEM HERE IS that many of the biblical archaeologists writing on this topic are cherry picking which ancient authors they will believe and accept. They do this inspite of the negative influences that could have motivated those authors to write what they did.

• • • •

WITHOUT THE ABILITY to verify, there words of extant ancient authors should not be allowed to be the only witness to an ancient people that were the enemy of the writers and their countries.

• • • •

THE INSCRIPTIONS ARE not clear

• • • •

THIS IS A VERY IMPORTANT issue in this discussion. Without any extra burial manuscripts, it is impossible to decipher what was in the minds of the ancient people when they wrote the inscriptions. At best, their words are merely their own belief in their own god and nothing more.

• • • •

THEY WERE BURIED THERE between the 8th century B.C. and the fall of Carthage during the third Punic War in 146 B.C. On the burial monuments that sometimes accompanied the urns, there was often inscribed the name or symbol of the goddess Tanit, the main Phoenician female deity, and her consort Ba'al Hammon. Infants and children were regularly sacrificed to this divine couple (#6).

• • • •

AGAIN, INSCRIPTIONS, when they are very general in nature and limited in data, are very vulnerable and can be manipulated into saying what the archaeologist wants it to say.

• • • •

THEN WHILE THERE MAY have been one or two inscriptions written by parents that actually may infer that their child was sacrificed it is not right to extrapolate that attitude to the whole city of inhabitants and throughout the city's history.

• • • •

DR. STAGER AND GREEN make mention of this fact when they wrote:

• • • •

EVIDENCE FROM PHOENICIAN inscriptions. What have come down to us are thousands of Phoenician inscriptions, the vast majority of which are from the Carthage Tophet. These inscriptions, however, are highly formulaic and tantalizingly laconic. None refers explicitly to child sacrifice, only to vows made to Tanit and Ba'al Hammon (#7).

· · · · ·

YET FOR SOME REASON they do not let this fact influence their conclusions in any way. The archaeologists and those who followed them continue to accept that the burnt remains of the different infants only point to child sacrifice and not to the idea that cremation may have been necessary as space was limited in the cemetery.

· · · ·

USING THE DENSITY OF urns in our excavated area as a standard, we estimate that as many as 20,000 urns may have been deposited there between 400 and 200 B.C. Clearly the deposits were not a casual or sporadic occurrence.

· · · ·

And

· · · ·

Later, when Carthage was flourishing along the shores of the Gulf of Tunis and the population of the metropolitan area probably exceeded a quarter of a million (Strabo† says 700,000), the demographic situation created little pressure for animal substitution. (#8).

· · · ·

THE CITY IS KNOWN TO have existed for about 600 years approx. prior to its final defeat. In that time millions of babies must have been born and more than 20,000 would have died during that time period.

• • • •

CREMATION MAY HAVE been a way to solve the space problem. This is a logical, rational, and acceptable explanation for the burned bodies. There is no reason to leap to a conclusion that child sacrifice was done whole-heartedly or on a very large scale.

• • • •

WITH THE LACK OF RECORDS from Carthage itself, we cannot say what laws were in force throughout those centuries. To assume that no laws governing the practice or outlawing child sacrifice were in place is an argument from silence.

• • • •

ANCIENT EXTANT AUTHORS would not and have not recorded any laws thus their accusations are suspicious to say the best about them.

• • • •

ACCORDING TO LEGEND, Carthage was founded by the Phoenician Queen Elissa (better known as Dido) sometime around 813 BCE... (#9).

• • • •

WHEN SHE FLED CANAAN, who is to say she did not outlaw the practice of child sacrifice? She was a woman and a woman of authority so it is more reasonable that she may have looked down on the practice. It cannot be assumed, given her story and history, that she brought those practices with her. Especially when there are no contemporary records saying what took place and what laws were enacted when the city was founded.

• • • •

PEOPLE ALSO CHANGE thus it is possible that if she did, later generations could have outlawed child sacrifice or enacted laws that permitted it. Without real, verifiable records from the people of Carthage there is no way to tell what actually took place in that city.

• • • •

THE MODERN ARCHAEOLOGIST cannot read long dead minds nor can he or she tell what took place in the past to any degree of certainty. That includes when the city and its records were destroyed over 2000 years ago.

• • • •

THE TEST OF TIME IS harsh and even if some records were still around during Tertullian's time they are lost now and his words cannot be verified either. This is a big problem as no new records, books, letters and so on have been found in the intervening years since Drs. Stager and Wolff excavated the city.

• • • •

IN OTHER WORDS, THERE is no new data to analyze. This brings this chapter to its next issue on this topic.

• • • •

ABORTION AND CHILD sacrifice

• • • •

THE MODERN BIBLICAL archaeologist cannot let modern personal preferences influence their study of past cultures.

• • • •

UNFORTUNATELY, THE good people at Associates of Biblical Research have let their disdain for abortion influence their views of the past. Those burnt bones found in those urns could easily have been babies from abortions committed by the women of Carthage.

• • • •

SINCE THERE ARE MANY parallels between ancient child sacrifice and modern abortion, it is reasonable to conclude that the attitude of our unchanging God towards abortion today is similar to His attitude towards child sacrifice in the past (#10).

• • • •

SOLOMON TELLS US THAT nothing new is under the sun (Ecc. 1) and abortion is not a modern phenomenon. It may be that the only real disposal method the people of Carthage had was by burning the aborted remains.

• • • •

THE TRUE STORY WILL never be known as modern archaeologist, including biblical ones, muddy the waters with their personal views. As for the remains of animals, there are also many reasons for their presence in the urns which will go unanswered forever.

• • • •

IT IS NOT RIGHT TO leap to conclusions about an ancient people and their practices when there is a large void of contemporary legitimate data to describe the events and daily lives of the people.

• • • •

THE ARGUMENT AGAINST scripture

• • • •

THIS POINT HAS BEEN raised and it is best to let the writer have his words be his own.

• • • •

MR. SMITH ADEPTLY REASONS that the arguments against a Tophet at Carthage will then be used to deny the biblical accounts relating such pagan sacrificial practices in the land of Canaan and Israel as outlined in OT Scripture (#11).

• • • •

THIS IS A VERY WEAK argument as God does not lie. What did or didn't happen in Carthage is not evidence for or against God and his word. If God said that the Israelites had forsaken him and sacrificed their children, then the ancient Israelites left God and followed the Canaanite gods and sacrificed their children.

• • • •

EVEN IF THE TOPHET in Carthage turns out to be a real cemetery for babies and their favorite pets, etc., that has no bearing on what took place approx., 1500 miles to the east in Israel.

• • • •

WHILE THE ISRAELITE falling away is evidence that the Canaanites in their region practiced child sacrifice, it is not really evidence to support what that Tophet in Carthage is said to represent.

• • • •

PLUS, UNBELIEVERS WILL use anything against the Bible. It doesn't matter if they use that Tophet in Carthage to say Jeremiah was wrong because believers know differently. The unbelievers' arguments do not change the truth.

• • • •

WHAT DOES MATTER IS if the biblical archaeologist is honest enough to look at the evidence and say what really took play or if they are brave enough to say 'we do not know' when it comes to child sacrifice in that city.

• • • •

AND ONE EVENT FOR ONE calamity does not taint the other 600 +/- years of that city's existence.

• • • •

CONCLUSION

• • • •

THE BIBLICAL ARCHAEOLOGIST must look at ancient societies, their evidence or lack of it under the influence of God's rules. The Bible says not to judge nor condemn for those are actions God has reserved for himself.

• • • •

WHAT THAT MEANS IS that we are not in a position to condemn the people of Carthage if they did practice child sacrifice as the record of the individual biblical archaeologist may not be holy in God's eyes either.

• • • •

THE BIBLICAL ARCHAEOLOGIST cannot read long dead minds nor can they apply the actions of a few to the many for there is no evidence supporting such a move. Also, the biblical archaeologist must be honest when looking at all the evidence.

• • • •

GOD DOES NOT LIE NOR can the biblical archaeologist. If there is a future for biblical archaeology, then its participants need to humble themselves and follow God's ways. For that is the only way to get to the truth. No matter where it lies.

• • • •

WORKS CITED

• • • •

#1. SMITH, HB, (2020), "Redeeming the Carthaginians?", Associates for Biblical Research, retrieved from https://biblearchaeology.org/research/contemporary-issues/4627-redeeming-the-carthaginians?highlight=WyJjYXJ0aGFnaSJd

#2. Vine, W. E. (1996). Collected writings of W.E. Vine. Nashville, TN: Thomas Nelson

#3. Stager, LE, & Greene, JA, (2004), "Were living Children Sacrificed to the Gods?", Archaeology Odyssey, 3(6).

#4. Ibid

#5. Ibid

#6. White, A., (2012), "Abortion and the Ancient Practice of Child Sacrifice", Associates for Biblical Archaeology, retrieved from https://biblearchaeology.org/research/contemporary-issues/2243-abortion-and-the-ancient-practice-of-child-sacrifice?highlight=WyJjYXJ0aGFnaSJd

#7. Op cit Stager & Greene (2004)

#8. Stager, LE & Wolff, SR, (1984), "Child Sacrifice at Carthage—Religious Rite or Population Control?", BAR, 10(1)

#9. Mark, J. J. (2018, May 14). Carthage. Ancient History Encyclopedia. Retrieved from https://www.ancient.eu/carthage/

#10. White, A., (2020), "Ancient Child Sacrifice and Abortion", Associates for Biblical Research, retrieved from https://biblearchaeology.org/research/contemporary-issues/4623-ancient-child-sacrifice-and-abortion?highlight=WyJjYXJ0aGFnZSJd

#11. Lanser, S., (2012), "Tanit in the Mirror: The Worship of Self and the Slaughter of Children ", Associates for Biblical Research, retrieved from https://biblearchaeology.org/research/contemporary-issues/4059-tanit-in-the-mirror-the-worship-of-self-and-the-slaughter-of-children?highlight=WyJjYXJ0aGFnZSJd

INTRODUCTION

• • • •

THE ISSUE OF SODOM is included in this work because if Biblical Archaeology is going to have a future, then the leadership and the example for quality, honest archaeological work falls squarely on the shoulders of those archaeologists and biblical scholars who are Christian.

• • • •

ONE CANNOT EXPECT THE unbelieving archaeologist, etc., to be honest, to follow God's rules or even represent God's word fairly. When Christian counterparts to those unbelieving professionals follow secular rules, secular strategies and do not follow God's ways then Biblical Archaeology is not going to have a future at all.

• • • •

IN THE CASE OF SODOM, there are archaeologists etc., who claim to be Christian who ignore what God has said and have set forth a bad example. They have only confused the issue for whatever reason they may have.

• • • •

TO EFFECTIVELY DEAL with this issue, this section is divided up into two parts. The first part will look at the three locations that have been proposed for the location of Sodom. Having more than one location does present some confusion as the extra locations take the persons' eyes off God and the truthfulness of his word.

• • • •

THE SECOND PART WILL look at one Christian archaeologist's point of view about Sodom. He is the lead archaeologist and has written at least one book on his personal choice for the location of Sodom.

• • • •

IT IS IMPORTANT TO respond to these points even though they were written about 10 years ago because the archaeologist has not changed his views and these points provide an excellent example when Christian archaeologists err and make things worse for God and his word.

• • • •

MISTAKES CAN BE EMBARRASSING

• • • •

WHEN LOOKING FOR THE location of any biblical city or geographical location, the biblical archaeologist has to be very careful. Mistakes can remove credibility from their reputation and render anything constructive or valuable they say later as nonsensical.

• • • •

IN OTHER WORDS, THE audience that you hope will listen to what the biblical archaeologist has to say will turn a deaf ear when it has been discovered that the biblical archaeologist was very wrong.

• • • •

ONE EXAMPLE OF THIS taking place was the supposed 2010 discovery of Noah's ark. The ministry that claimed they had made a discovery of wooden compartments in 2007 & 2008. Their announcement surprised the world but when the proper evidence was not revealed, very little was heard from that group or their supposed discovery again. That is no surprise given that they had embarrassed themselves very badly and made anything they said suspect (#1).

· · · · ·

IF THE BIBLICAL ARCHAEOLOGIST does come across something that is unique or as historical as discovering Noah's Ark, they are going to have to be very sure of the identification before announcing it to the world.

· · · · ·

THIS DOES NOT MEAN there won't be skeptics who reject the identification but if done correctly and it is the truth, then the biblical archaeologist will not be the one embarrassed.

· · · · ·

EVEN WHEN EILAT MAZAR made claims of discovering King David's palace, there were detractors. She followed all the protocols but that did not stop Israel Finkelstein and others from writing a paper opposing her identification (#2).

· · · · ·

THE KEY IS TO HAVE all the right information and make sure it is the truth first. Words like 'we believe...' or 'it is possible...' and similar sentence structures does not do anything for anyone but simply state the personal views of the biblical archaeologist.

· · · · ·

SUCH TERMS ARE USED, of course, to make sure if proven wrong no damage is done to the reputation of the scholar. But it is far better to say 'we or I don't know...' than to make claims about a discovery that cannot be supported by evidence or verified by other scholars or archaeologists.

· · · ·

IT ISN'T EMBARRASSMENT that is the only issue here. One's testimony, evangelistic and other gospel efforts are also affected when a biblical archaeologist makes big claims like those supposed ark discoverers.

· · · ·

THAT MESSAGE AND THOSE efforts must be protected at all times. They won't be effective if the biblical archaeologist has made some claims that end up being wild ideas influenced by their Christian beliefs. Or they end up harming the efforts of other believers as guilt by association is not a stranger to believers.

· · · ·

THERE IS ONE SAVING grace when mistakes of location are made, it is very hard to determine exact historical locations. Even signs like this, Sodom would be suspect, as the sign could have been made at any time in human history and placed at different ancient sites.

· · · ·

THERE IS NO DOUBT THAT the "Cities of the Plain" were located in the southern Ghor. This is the irresistible conclusion of the combined evidence from the Rast-Schaub survey and from Ebla. What remains to be established is which site was which city. Albright's location of Sodom at the end of the Wadi Numeira is attractive. That would mean that Sodom is Numeira. Yet there are difficulties which prevent such an identification, and which indeed suggest that Sodom is Feifeh (#3).

. . . .

AS YOU CAN SEE EVEN professionals have a very hard time in identifying an ancient site. Mistakes will be made, and it will be up to how the biblical archaeologist and how they handle the problem whether there is any fall out or not.

. . . .

THERE WILL BE CONFUSION as archaeology can only go by the evidence it uncovers and when cities have similar or no evidence identification is next to impossible. Sodom is one of those problem locations that confuse people and harms the gospel outreach of believers.

. . . .

WHERE IS SODOM

. . . .

CURRENTLY THERE ARE 2 main locations that different archaeologists have claimed to be Sodom or the Cities of the Plain. 2 are not accurate although one of those two is fairly close to the one that is most likely the location of both Sodom and Gomorrah.

. . . .

ALBRIGHT HAD ATTRIBUTED the absence of earlier evidence of settlements to the fact that ancient Zoar was now covered by waters of the southern Dead Sea (#4).

. . . .

THIS IS THE FIRST LOCATION that held any merit for locating Sodom. The region was correct, down near the southern part of the

Dead Sea but instead of [placing the cities on land Dr. Albright and others felt that the Sea expanded and covered the plain.

• • • •

THE LACK OF SUPPORTING evidence to the traditional identification of es-Sefi with Zoar, along with the absence of inhabited sites along the wadis leading to the Dead Sea, led Albright and others to the conclusion that the "Cities of the Plain" were located in the southern basin of the Dead Sea itself (#5).

• • • •

THERE IS GOOD REASON for this conclusion as the Dead Sea was known to raise and lower its water levels depending on the season of the year and how much rainfall took place in any given year.

• • • •

ONE THING ABOUT THE Dead Sea is certain: Its water level has fluctuated considerably over the millennia. When the water level is relatively low, the southern basin of the lake dries up, exposing the shelf underneath. When the water level rises, the southern shelf is submerged and the shoreline around the lake is higher. Any structure, such as a port built on the edge of the lake during periods of low water levels, would then be under water. When the water subsides again, the port would again be exposed—and so would the southern shelf (#6).

• • • •

THE RISING WATERS WOULD cover much of the destroyed valley hiding God's judgment whenever the waters were high enough. Then God's judgment would be revealed whenever the waters of the Dead Sea lowered.

• • • •

IT MAKES SENSE TO THOSE who cannot find the right location for Sodom as the destructive layer would be uninhabitable even when the waters lowered. The salt in the Dead Sea would take care of any fertile soil.

. . . .

BUT THE PROBLEM WITH this location is that Sodom and area were left as an example to all who lived ungodly lives from the destruction forward (See 2 Peter 2:6). The area could not be seen if it were buried underwater and never seen.

. . . .

THE SECOND LOCATION is identified as Bab edh-Dhra and Numeria region which is a very desolate geographical area on the south eastern side of the Dead Sea.

. . . .

ONE POPULAR THEORY, repeated yet today, is that the Cities of the Plain were located in the plain south of the Dead Sea and later covered by the waters of the southern basin, never to be seen again. The level of the Dead Sea has receded substantially in recent years, causing the southern basin to dry up.2 Extensive exploration and activity in the area has produced no evidence to indicate that there were ancient sites there (Rast 1987a: 193).

. . . .

RAST AND SCHAUB DISCOVERED four additional sites south of Bab edh-Dhra, which they suggested might be related to the Cities of the Plain of the Old Testament (Rast and Schaub 1974). Subsequent excavations at Numeira, 13 km (8 mi) south of Bab edh-Dhra, have verified its close affinity with Bab edh-Dhra (7#).

• • • •

THIS REGION HAS NOT changed in the past 20 years. Subsequent excavations have provided more data on the destruction and the lack of habitation. It has also shown that the area was once very habitable and well-watered (#8). But that is not the only physical evidence that has been uncovered at these sites.

• • • •

IF YOU RECALL THE STORY of Sodom in the time of Abraham, Sodom, and Gomorrah were attacked by a king and his army because the rulers of both Sodom, Gomorrah and other cities refused to pay tribute, etc (Genesis 14).

• • • •

THIS MEANS THAT ANY ancient site being regarded as Sodom or Gomorrah must show this destruction, as well as the final one.

• • • •

IN ITS RELATIVELY SHORT period of occupation Numeira underwent two destructions. The final destruction is particularly evident from excavation of the residential area. The evidence for the earlier destruction of the town comes especially from the eastern end of the town where the defensive tower was built (#9).

• • • •

BESIDES ALL THE PHYSICAL evidence that stands out for Bab edh-Dhrah and Numeria as Sodom and Gomorrah, the region fits the description in 2 Peter 2. it is easily seen, people can visit there if they wish and they will be reminded of God's judgment on the ungodly.

• • • •

THIS IS THE KEY. LOCATION must fit God's description for the city or it is probably not the correct site. Try as one might to fit the ancient location into God's word it won't work unless all the elements are in place.

• • • •

THAT IS THE PROBLEM with the 3rd main location Tall el-Hamman. Its identification and progress over the years can be found at the many pages of the website dedicated to that excavation, tallelhamman.com.

• • • •

WHETHER IT IS FORTUNATE or not, Dr. S. Collins is not the originator of this identification. A French archaeologist proposed the northern location long before Dr. Collins thought of the site and made it popular (#10). The difference being Dr. Collins fervently defends his identification of Tall el-Hamman as Sodom.

• • • •

HE MAY USE THE BIBLE to help him locate the doomed city in his northern region, but the Bible does not back up his claims especially 2 Peter 2. Then there is the problem of the two destructions. Tall el-Hamman has been said, by Dr. Collins and others who have dug at his site that there has been only 1 destruction found (#11).

• • • •

THIS IS NOT THE ONLY drawback that excludes this site from being Sodom. The destructive layer was buried and did not meet the word of the Apostle Peter that it would be an example to all the ungodly. The word 'thereafter' in the New Testament book does not have an end date to it. That means the destructive layer must be visible every day of the year in every year after the destruction took place.

· · · ·

YET THERE ARE MORE problems that occur with the 3rd location for Sodom and these problems cannot be ignored or dismissed. Those that support the 3rd location redefine the size of the Plain of Jordan to fit their theory. This is something that a biblical archaeologist cannot do even if it destroys their theory. Two quotes to emphasize that the Jordan Plain is not as small as the supporters of the 3rd location want it to be:

· · · ·

IN THE OTHER DIRECTION the Dead Sea's catchment area stretches from the central ridge of Canaan as far east as the eastern flanks of the Transjordanian plateau. The catchment area thus encompasses about 11,000 square miles (#12).

· · · ·

AND

· · · ·

MAZAR SUGGESTS THAT the border included these parts of southern Transjordan based on Gen 10:9, which defines the borders of Canaan with the markers of the "cities of the plain" (e.g., Sodom and Gomorrah) that were presumably located on the southeastern end of the Dead Sea (#13).

· · · ·

THE ERRORS MADE HERE do provide some embarrassment to those who support the 3rdlocation as Sodom but there is one more important point that Dr.Collins and Tall el-Hamman supporters ignore and at least they have not talked about it.

. . . .

THIS ERROR COMES FROM their assessment that Sodom lay along the East West trade route that passed by Jericho. Yet there is a problem with that assessment. Two major ancient roads were found one going north south along the Dead Sea's eastern shore and one that went east west and went over part of the southern portion of the Dead Sea.

. . . .

BOTH ARCHAEOLOGY AND Arab tradition indicate that at some time in the past one could walk, ride, or drive from the peninsula (el-Lisan) across to what is now the west shore of the Dead Sea. In an aerial survey made with an officer of the British Flying Force, Nelson Glueck was able to trace the greater part of the old Roman road which ran from the mountain plateau of Moab through el-Moteh and Kathrabba in a northwesterly direction toward the Lisan (Fig. 8). This road in a sense connected two great Roman highways, one of which ran through Kerak (Biblical Kir) in Moab southwards to the Gulf of Akabah and the other from near the southeast corner of the Lisan southward along the east shore of the Dead Sea and the east side of the Arabah to Aila on the Gulf of Akabah (#14).

. . . .

WHAT THIS MEANS IS that there was a road to Bab edh-Drah region prior to the destruction of the cities of the plain. One which the King could easily use to attack those 5 cities for their rebellion.

. . . .

THERE WERE OTHER MAIN roads through the region making it possible for the residents, including Lot to conduct business with travelers and fulfill Ezekiel 16:49. The cities did not have to be in the northern location because they were already well situated for travel and trade along these major roads.

• • • •

LOT DID NOT HAVE TO cross the Jordan to get to Sodom as there was a perfectly good road for him to use, if he used main trade routes to move his livestock away from Abraham's flocks.

• • • •

GLUECK THINKS THAT a branch of the west road (that along the east shore of the Dead Sea) ran to the Lisan and across this peninsula to the Dead Sea; "it then probably crossed to the west side of the Dead Sea over the ford which used to be passable from the Lisan to the other side". In 1924, Dr. Kyle came upon this western Roman road and also a Roman milestone south of Lisan. He noted the branch which forked to the northwest and ran "right down the centre of the Lisan to the point where it reaches the narrow, deep gorge on the western side". This, with other evidence which cannot be discussed here, indicates that there was a Roman road across the Lisan which forded the Sea (#15).

• • • •

CONCLUSION

• • • •

FINDING THE ERRORS before promoting a location as a site for biblical events and cities is important. One cannot let ego get in the way of being corrected. The biblical archaeologist must follow God's rules and be honest about their conclusions and identifications.

• • • •

THEY MUST ALSO BE PREPARED to make changes and stay in line with what God has said. That means the biblical archaeologist must full and correctly understand the biblical texts they are working with.

. . . .

USING GOD'S WORD TO justify their claims and excavation site is the same as using people to meet one's objectives. It is not right, and it brings God's word into question, turning people away from God because they cannot trust a Supreme Being who can't even get his own story correct.

. . . .

THERE IS NO DOUBT THAT the Bab edh-Dhra region is the area for the cities of the plain. While the location under the dead Sea is close and could very well be part of the destroyed plain, it is not the sole location for the cities.

. . . .

THE 3RD LOCATION IS just erroneous and misleading causing confusion among believers and unbelievers alike. In the old BAS forum that existed back in the early first decade of the 21st century, both Dr. Collins and Dr. Graves made a statement that questioned the Bab edh-Drha location as Sodom. They asked why would anyone build cities and reside in such a desolate area.

. . . .

THEY WERE DRAWING CONCLUSIONS looking at the land after it was destroyed and not as the land was before that judgment took place. That is a mistake that a biblical archaeologist cannot afford to make.

. . . .

THEY HAVE TO MAKE SURE they know the scripture and apply it to their excavation site correctly.

Works Cited

• • • •

#1. THAN, K., (2010), "Noah's Ark Found in Turkey", National Geographic, retrieved from https://www.nationalgeographic.com/news/2010/4/100428-noahs-ark-found-in-turkey-science-religion-culture/

#2. Finkelstein, I., et al, (2007), "Has King David's Palace in Jerusalem Been Found", Tel Aviv University

#3. van Hattem, W.C., (1981), "Once Again: Sodom and Gomorrah", Biblical Archaeologist, 44.

#4. Ibid

#5. Ibid

#6. Frumkin, A., and Elitzur, Y., (2001), "The Rise and Fall of the Dead Sea", BAR, 27(6).

#7. Wood, B. G. (1999). The Discovery of the Sin Cities of Sodom and Gomorrah. Bible and Spade, 12(3), 66.

#8. Ibid

#9. Shea, W. H. (1988). Numeirah. Bible and Spade, 1(4), 12.

#10 Harland, J.P., (2001), "Sodom and Gomorrah: The Location of the Cities of the Plain", Biblical Archaeologist 1-4, 5(electronic ed.).

#11. Collins, S., (2007), "Forty Salient Points on the Geography of the Cities of the Kikkar", BIBLICAL RESEARCH BULLETIN The Academic Journal of Trinity Southwest University ISSN 1938-694X Volume VII Number 1

#12 Bietzel, B.J. (2004), "The Dead Sea—background to the Bible", Bible Review, 3(3).

#13. McKinny, C. (2016). Zin, Wilderness of. In J. D. Barry, D. Bomar, D. R. Brown, R. Klippenstein, D. Mangum, C. Sinclair Wolcott, … W. Widder (Eds.), The Lexham Bible Dictionary. Bellingham, WA: Lexham Press.

#14. Op Cit Harland (2001)

#15. Ibid

Addressing the Forty Salient Points on the Geography of the Cities of the Kikkar

INTRODUCTION

• • • •

THE AUTHOR WHO WROTE the article of the same name as above will be noted only in the footnote as this chapter is not an attack on him. His words are used as an example because they reflect the wrong attitudes a biblical archaeologist should have.

• • • •

ALL THE QUOTES WILL be taken from that article so there will not be a long list of references at the end of this chapter. Bible verses will be listed, when used, in the text.

• • • •

ALSO, MANY OF THE OPPOSING points made in rebuttal to the few points we list here have all been said to the author directly years ago when The Biblical archaeological society had its own discussion forum.

• • • •

DUE TO THE SIMILAR nature of many of those 40 points and the limited space available here, not all of the 40 points will be addressed. Some can be lumped together while others will be excluded as they are nonsensical and do not further the discussion or are repetitive.

• • • •

IF BIBLICAL ARCHAEOLOGY has a future then the attitude of the biblical archaeologist should be in tune with what God has outlined in his word. There is no room for arrogance, and other sinful attitudes as the biblical archaeologist has more to worry about than just creating a theory or proving the validity of the Bible.

• • • • •

THEIR ATTITUDE MUST be in line with God's teaching so as not to put people off from salvation. At the same time, the biblical archaeologist cannot change what the Bible says, even through archaeological discoveries to keep people from being offended by the gospel and contents of the rest of the Bible.

• • • • •

PEOPLE WILL BE OFFENDED by the Bible no matter what discoveries come to light and how much they prove the Bible true. It is imperative that we search for the truth and proclaim that truth as Paul described in 1 Cor. 13.

• • • • •

#1. I HAVE ANALYZED the definitive text on Sodom's location (Gen 13:1-12) in extreme detail. (#1).

• • • • •

ONE SHOULD NOT BE SO quick to determine what is the definitive text on Sodom's location when it comes to the biblical verses. God doe snot always use very specific geographical markers when describing a city, a ruler and so on. That is because it is not the geographical location that is God's priority.

• • • • •

IT IS THE LESSON GOD is about to teach that takes precedence over location. When you read that self declared definitive description, you will note that there are very few geographical markers included in the passage. The key words would be in verse 10 and they are 'the whole valley of the Jordan and that is not enough to determine where Sodom was located.

. . . .

#2. I HAVE INVESTIGATED the chronological issues with a rigor, I believe, second to none.

. . . .

JESUS TALKED ABOUT how a man's own testimony is not true and while the author is trying to protect himself from future arguments, his testimony does not ring true as there are probably others in history who had access to more documents than he had who studied them better than he did.

. . . .

WE DO NOT NEED BRAGGING or arrogance in biblical archaeology. Those attitudes are not biblical, Christ serving or beneficial to the study of history or the Bible. It is accepted that he put a lot of study into the matter but so have many other professional archaeologists and bible students and insulting their efforts is not getting off on the right foot.

. . . .

#3. I HAVE READ VIRTUALLY every piece of literature from every period available on the subject. I have discussed/argued every conceivable point in the discussion with many of the world's leading scholars, both minimalists and maximalists, who are capable of interacting meaningfully on the issues involved. I have personally walked nearly every square meter of the geography and topography for all proposed Sodom sites. I have traversed the ancient trade routes of the region and surveyed every known archaeological site in it and adjacent to it...I have studied the reports of all excavated sites in the area, including the traditional "southern" ones. Perhaps I would even qualify as an expert on the subject of Sodom's location.

. . . .

HE MAY HAVE DONE ALL of that but those accomplishments are not the issue. Did you count all the 'I' in his declarations? There are far too many which tells us that the author is more about himself and not enough about God.

. . . .

IF WE ARE GOING TO go about God's work and use archaeology to prove the Bible true then we need to follow God and put him in the forefront instead of lifting oneself up and making it seem that the biblical archaeologist is doing this work on their own effort without the help of God.

. . . .

ALSO, JUST BECAUSE ONE has done all of the things listed in these opening points, still doe snot mean that he came to the correct answer. Before a biblical archaeologist speaks and makes announcements of finds, declarations of their work, they should at first make sure they are correct and have been led to the truth by God.

. . . .

#4. BY THIS POINT IN the process, it is safe to say that I have heard every conceivable argument for every Sodom candidate, and have dealt squarely and scientifically with every question and objection raised with regard to the identification of Tall el-Hammam as biblical Sodom.

. . . .

HE MAY CLAIM THIS BUT all it refers to is his unwillingness to listen to opposing points of view. There are key passages in the Bible that show that he is premature in his clams and that he has made several errors that have led him to the wrong site.

. . . .

HE MAY HAVE DEALT SCIENTIFICALLY with each argument, but again, that does not mean he is correct or got the right location. It just means he refuses to be told that he is wrong.

. . . .

#4. THE "SOUTHERN SODOM view" has had its day, but that day is drawing to a close, whether its advocates want to admit it or not.

. . . .

INSULTING THOSE OF opposing views is not the biblical archaeologist. Nor is it right to make determinations one does not have the authority to make. There are reasons why the southern view is more likely the spot for Sodom and it is because the evidence fits what God's word says.

. . . .

THE AUTHOR'S CALLING the supporter's proposed location in the Southern location fantasy is mocking those who disagree with his conclusion that Tall el Hamman is the site for Sodom. Biblical archaeologists let the truth make the determination not someone's personal viewpoint or preference.

. . . .

#5. STORY TELLERS AND writers in the ancient Near East did not invent fictitious geographies, but used what was known from personal experience, shared (cultural) experience, or "traditional" geographical wisdom, i.e., actual geography, whether phenomenological or formulaic.

· · · ·

HERE WE START WITH the 40 points the author has written to defend his conclusion that Tall el Hamman is Sodom. The first 4 points of his article and to say the least most of those 4 points are correct no matter where Sodom located. The 4th point lumped in with the other three is a moot point.

· · · ·

HAVING GEOGRAPHICAL markers does not lessen the value of the other passages of scripture nor elevate gen.13 1-12 to superiority status. The markers, if there really are any, needed to be put somewhere. Biblical archaeologists cannot overstate their information and make it out to be more than it really is.

· · · ·

#6. OUTSIDE THE OLD Testament, among the Semitic cognates and Egyptian, kikkar/kakkar/kakkaru/kerker is never used as a geographical referent, but means only a "talent, a flat, circular weight of metal" or "circular, flat loaf of bread"; in Egyptian there is also the meaning "to draw a circle in the sand with a stick."

· · · ·

THIS IS POINT #7 AND it represents points 6 to 11 as they all talk about this word kikkar' and its relationship to the passage in Genesis. The author makes a big deal on this as his use of the word and the definition he has chosen to use support his points and hypothesis.

· · · ·

YET, INSTEAD OF APPLYING the translation of the word correctly, the author manipulates it the word and its translation in order to have it support his point of view. The author limits the scope of the valley of the Jordan to what he wants it to be even though there is nothing in the text that directs one to make such a restriction.

· · · ·

THIS IS ALSO SOMETHING a biblical archaeologist can't do. They have to be honest and let the different Hebrew words represent what God had intended them to represent. There is nothing in the text that says this word kikkar applies to only the northern are above the Dead Sea. That concept is read into the word not taken out of it.

· · · ·

THERE ARE MANY GEOGRAPHICAL and translation arguments that would render the author's application as bad archaeology but those arguments deserve their own paper as there is not enough space here to do the job justice.

· · · ·

#7. THE TEXT SUGGESTS that Lot viewed with his "unaided" physical eyes the entire Jordan Disk from the area east of Bethel/Ai (above and W/NW of Jericho); the entire kikkar is, in fact, visible from the highland's edge east of Bethel/Ai (which I have personally viewed on many occasions).

· · · ·

YES, IT IS ACCEPTED that both Lot and Abraham may not have had binoculars or telescopes to view the valley but they were not needed as the passage does not state that they saw every square inch of the plain.

• • • •

THE PASSAGE SAYS 'LOT saw that the valley was well watered' one does not have to see every inch to to see the reality of having a well watered area to graze one's flocks. It is an assumption also, that the pair were staring all the way north to almost Jerusalem. We do not know the full extent of their gaze or the exact direction they were looking in.

• • • •

#8. LOT TRAVELED EASTWARD from Bethel/Ai, pitching his tent toward Sodom, one of the cities of the eastern Jordan Disk, while Abram remained "in Canaan"; i.e., Lot went east of the Jordan River beyond the formulaic Canaan boundary, remaining north of the Dead Sea all the while, no doubt traveling along the convenient E/W trade route that passed near Jericho, then crossed the river to the cities on the far side of the alluvial plain—the Cities of the Kikkar.

• • • •

THERE ARE AT LEAST 2 things wrong with this point. First, the author resorts to possibilities and not fact. And he misunderstands the directional marker because he knows little of driving a herd of livestock.

• • • •

IT IS NOT KNOWN HOW powerful or how swift the current the Jordan had in Abraham's time. Some experts say it was fairly powerful. This fact tells us that Lot would have to find a safe place to bring his livestock across if he did what the author assumes.

• • • •

BUT VERSE 11 IN GENESIS 13 only states in the NASB that Lot journeyed to the East. It does not say that he crossed the Jordan river.

The NIV states that Lot 'set out towards the east' implying that he did not continue in an Easterly route but may have turned south before reaching the Jordan or possibly turning south and going around the southern end of the Dead Sea.

• • • •

THERE IS NO GEOGRAPHICAL marker letting us know if he went due east the whole time. Lot, being a rancher, would have taken the best route for his livestock and that may not necessarily mean crowding the other travelers on the east west trade route.

• • • •

IF ANYONE KNOWS ANYTHING about cattle drives, the owner takes the route that has the most food and water for his flock and that wouldn't be a trade route.

• • • •

#9. SODOM WAS ONE OF the Cities of the Plain (kikkar = disk). No city south of the mouth of hayarden would have been considered as belonging to the Jordan Disk or the cities thereof.

• • • •

THIS QUOTE REPRESENTS the author's points from 14 to 22 and deal with the location of Sodom and the Age the cities were in when the destruction came. The author's conclusions are all mere assumptions made to keep his theory intact and viable. There is nothing in any of the passages that puts Sodom near Jericho or Jerusalem.

• • • •

THEN THE DATING OF the Age Sodom was in is also moot as that is very subjective and very difficult to do. When the cities came into existence and how long they were around is not important to either the account or the destruction.

• • • •

WHAT IS IMPORTANT IS that the destruction took place when God said it did and the Biblical Archaeologist needs to believe that. Those approx. 8 to 9 points are mere distractions and have little to do with the account.

• • • •

THE DATES AND ORIGINATION do not support the northern location as even that site's origination is up for debate and vulnerable to a variety of subjective opinions.

• • • •

#10. THE CITY OF SODOM itself was fortified.

• • • •

WE KNOW THIS BECAUSE the angels of the Lord found Lot sitting in the gate of the city. But being fortified does not tell us anything about the design of the gate, the size of the city or the city's importance. It only speaks to the concerns of the inhabitants in that they wanted to have some protection from attacks.

• • • •

#11. GIVEN A MBA DATE for Abram, archaeologically and geographically speaking, the largest fortified Bronze Age urban center on the eastern Jordan Disk would be a "most likely" candidate for biblical Sodom.

• • • •

NOT NECESSARILY AS we are never told how big the cities of the plain were. It is mere assumption and a desperate attempt to fortify an alternative northern location theory. Sodom was the size it was and God did not think that its size was important or vital for us to know.

. . . . .

EVEN IF IT WAS LARGE, it didn't stop the destruction from taking place.

. . . . .

#12. AN OCCUPATIONAL hiatus of several centuries after a fiery MBA destruction would make that "Sodom" identification almost irresistible (in the time of Moses and Joshua the eastern Jordan Disk is called "the wasteland" below Pisgah—Num 21:20).

. . . . .

THIS MAY BE SO BUT that wilderness was not in the region where the author claims his location for Sodom resides. In fact, during the time of Moses when the people of Gad and Reuban came to collect their inheritance of the promised land, they found the eastern side of the Jordan river, to be perfect for their livestock.

. . . . .

REUBAN'S LAND WAS RIGHT next to the northern section of the Dead Sea and Gad's was just above his covering the author's location with fertile land (Numbers 32:1). Then what Peter said about the area surrounding Sodom was that it was to be an example forever (2 Peter 2:6). A destroyed land cannot be an example if it is buried under fertile land. It would be a testament for God's mercy and forgiveness but not as an example to what happens to those who disobey God.

. . . . .

#13. SOUTHERN DEAD SEA sites, such as Bab edh-Dhra and Numeira, satisfy not a single "Cities of the Plain" criterion set forth in the Genesis 13 narrative (summarized in Points 20, 23-27 above) because (a) they were destroyed at the end of the EBA centuries before the time of Abram and Lot (given a Middle Bronze Age date for Abram); and (b) they are entirely in the wrong place (whether or not the tales are factual or etiological, and regardless of date!

• • • •

THIS IS JUST WRONG. The southern location of Bab edh-Dhra and Numeria fulfill all of the criterion that identifies Sodom to be in that location. Also, there are several additional criterion that the author just ignores.

• • • •

FOR EXAMPLE, MT SODOM is located near the southern location and not even close to the northern location (#2). When evidence goes contrary to the theory or personal preference of the biblical archaeologist, the biblical archaeologist needs to be honest in analyzing those pieces of evidence and readjust their theory.

• • • •

NOT MAKE EXCUSE FOR why it does not fit or ignoring them. Tall el Hamman has no local or historical markers that indicate Sodom was there.

• • • •

#14. THE SODOM NARRATIVE carefully marks out a location for the cities of the Kikkar north of the Dead Sea on the east bank of the Jordan River where, in fact, the ruins of significant Bronze and Iron Age cities exist. Such a high degree of correspondence between text and ground cannot be mere coincidence.

. . . .

THIS POINT COVERS THE rest that have not been covered from about 27 to 40 as most of those are mere declarations without fact or evidence to support their claims. All the northern location has going for it are the assumptions and possibilities read into the text to give the author's theory some credibility.

. . . .

A CLOSE EXAMINATION shows that the author is grasping at straws and hopes to diminish opposition by browbeating his opponents with no facts just information he reads into his definitive passage.

. . . .

SOME FINAL WORDS

. . . .

THE ARGUMENT THAT BAB ed-Dhrah is not the location fails because of one main fact. God told us through peter that the area would remain a wasteland forever. If you read the excavation reports for Tall el-Hamman you will see that the author of this article clearly states that there was a destruction layer that lasted only about 500 years (#3).

. . . .

THAT FACT UNCOVERED by the author excludes and eliminates the northern location from consideration for the location of Sodom. All the so called evidence supporting the author's declaration and conclusion do not support his claims.

. . . .

MOST OF THE EVIDENCE shown by the author is excludes information that disqualifies the location, does not support the location, and products of great misunderstanding as well as being arguments from silence.

• • • •

EVEN THE 40 POINTS the author constructed do not save his identification as they do not pinpoint any objective piece of evidence that supports his claim. For the biblical archaeologist this cannot be done.

• • • •

THE CHRISTIAN ARCHAEOLOGIST has eternity as a factor and they must be correct if they want to make an impact for God. The location of Sodom is not just about locating the cities of destruction.

• • • •

IT IS ABOUT PRESENTING an honest testimony that brings glory to God while showing his word to be true. The biblical archaeologist represents God not themselves or their theory and they mus be ready to be corrected when they make errors, especially ones this large.

• • • •

WORKS CITED

• • • •

#1. COLLINS, S., (2007), "Forty Salient Points on the Geography of the Cities of the Kikkar", BIBLICAL RESEARCH BULLETIN The Academic Journal of Trinity Southwest University ISSN 1938-694X Volume VII Number 1, retrieved from http://nebula.wsimg.com/ 062ff508dfc71e6ffcdb1ee72f356fc2?AccessKeyId=AD0C503627C3B88

#2. Dead Sea.com (2019), "Mount Sodom, & Lot's Wife", https://www.deadsea.com/explore/historical-sites/biblical-sites/mount-sodom-lots-wife/

#3. The Tall el Hamman Excavation Project https://trinitysouthwest.com/dig/

THERE ARE ALWAYS MYSTERIES

. . . .

ARCHAEOLOGY MAY SOLVE some problems the Christian world needs answered about the Bible but due to its limited nature that field of research cannot answer them all. One of those mysteries concerns the the identity of the Hyksos.

. . . .

ACCORDING TO MOST EGYPTOLOGISTS and other archaeologists, the Hyksos were invaders of Egypt somewhere between the 12th and the 16th Dynasties. Their appearance has been held to that time as there are few ancient manuscripts whose contents refer to that group of people . They are also scattered, lacking in detail and so on (#1).

. . . .

THIS PAPER IS NOT GOING to deal with the location of their capital or call into question the work of Dr. Manfred Bietak who has dug at the Hyksos capital of Avaris for over 40 years. Instead it is going to call into question the timeline, which Dr. David Rohl has already done with his new chronology (#2).

. . . .

THE EGYPTIAN PHARAOH Timeline

. . . .

WHEN ONE READS THE book Egyptian Art published by Phaidon they get a very detailed analysis of Egyptian life and the artwork surrounding the different pharaohs that reigned over Egypt.

. . . .

IN THE BACK OF THE book there is a rather detailed chronology listing all of the different pharaohs except for a couple of dynasties. There are many names missing from the 13th to 17th dynasty as those names may be lost to history.

. . . .

BUT WHAT IS STRIKING are the words at the top of the page. Those words read- "all dates before the seventh century BC should be regarded as approximate. The margin of error varies from some one hundred years..." (#3).

. . . .

IT MAY NOT BE THE SCHOLAR'S fault for this discrepancy, it could be that Egyptian records do not follow legitimate chronological rules or historical requirements. This is something about the ancient Egyptians.

. . . .

THEY WERE KNOWN TO alter their history to make future generations more patriotic, to make those early generations look good, powerful and wise. Even the records recorded in stone cannot be trusted as there is no way to know if they were not edited after their initial inscribing (#4).

. . . .

WITH THE LACK OF DOCUMENTS referring to the Hyksos it is also impossible to fully verify what has been said about them and their place in Egyptian history. Since very little is known of this people it is possible that their place in the Egyptian chronology is erroneous and may be applied to a later date.

• • • •

THE MANY KING'S LISTS

• • • •

THE PROBLEM ISN'T JUST with the lack of manuscripts discussing the Hyksos, there are problems with the many different king's lists that Egyptologists have used to determine the order of Pharaohs and when they reigned.

• • • •

PROBABLY THE BEST KING'S list is the Royal Canon of Turin. When discovered it contained almost all or part of 222 different names of Pharaohs who ruled. The problem with this list is that since its discovery, over 2/3 of the document has disintegrated, no good photos were taken and no real scientific examination has been done on the papyrus (#5).

• • • •

WITH SO MUCH INFORMATION lost it is hard to construct a proper order for all of the kings who ruled Egypt. Part of the solution came from the Abydos, The Saqqara and the Karnak king's list. There are issues with those lists as well as as the two former lists were not designed to be a chronological compilation. Like Karnak, Saqqara did not list all the kings and Karnak listed names of Pharaohs that appeared on no other list (#6).

• • • •

THERE ARE OTHER PROBLEMS with these lists and those issues tend to make determining the correct order or rulers, including the Hyksos, very difficult. There is no document tying those king's list together or showing how they are connected. They each may have a different purpose, like the Saqqra list which was supposed to be made honoring ancestors. The lack of connection makes discovering the different rules very difficult (#7).

• • • •

THERE IS ALWAYS MANETHO

• • • •

MANETHO LIVED DURING the 30tth Dynasty and wrote his history for the Greek rulers who came to power after Alexander the Great conquered the land. His three volume history of Egypt, called the Aegyptiaca, has not survived except by quotations in other ancient author's works. It was this work that helped divide the ancient pharaohs into 30 dynasties (#8).

• • • •

BUT AS STATED, THERE is so little known about Manetho. And what makes matters worse is that his 3 volume history does not survive except through different quotations:

• • • •

"WE CAN KNOW HIS WRITINGS only from fragmentary and often distorted quotations preserved chiefly by Josephus and by the Christian chronographers, Africanus and Eusebius, with isolated passages in Plutarch, Theophilus, Aelian, Porphyrius, Diogenes

Laertius, Theodoretus, Lydus, Malalas, the Scholia to Plato, and the Etymologicum Magnum." (#9).

. . . .

THE IMPORTANT PASSAGE about the Hyksos is found in Josephus and to quote from his work:

. . . .

"IN HIS REIGN, FOR WHAT cause I know not, a blast of God smote us; and unexpectedly, from the regions of the East, invaders of obscure race marched in confidence of victory against our land. By main force they easily seized it without striking a blow;4 and having overpowered the rulers of the land, they then burned our cities ruthlessly, razed to the ground the temples of the gods, and treated all the natives with a cruel hostility, massacring some and leading into slavery the wives and children of others." (#10).

. . . .

THE ONLY REAL TIME that this could have taken place was after the Pharaoh and his army were destroyed during the Exodus. While it is quite possible that the Hyksos could have come to power through non military means, like Joseph had, that does not seem probable as they would have had to have complete control over the Egyptian military and other high offices to make the coup work and it is hard to consider the Egyptian army rebelling against their own people in favor of foreigners. Among other obstacles.

. . . .

SINCE THE HYKSOS PRESENCE in Northern Egypt has been referred to as an invasion, there really is not record of any invasion of Egypt during the 13th or 14th dynasties that would explain their entering the land (#11).

• • • •

EGYPT WAS NOT A WEAK nation until the Exodus took place making it possible for an invading force to take the land without, as Manetho describes, striking a blow. Their army was gone as was their Pharaoh and reeling from all the plagues including the loss of the first born, the people of Egypt were not in the frame of mind or position to defend their land.

• • • •

AHMOSE I MAY HAVE EXPELLED the Hyksos as the Rhind papyrus has mentioned but it is possible that it was after his stated rule of 1550 to 1525 BC. (#12). Because of the sparsity of records it is hard to say and theories do abound.

• • • •

ONE MUST BE CAUTIOUS when using Manetho because he was commissioned by Ptolemy II to write the histories and given Egyptian mentality, Manetho could have changed Egyptian history to make the country seem better than it was (#13). Without copies of his original work it can never be certain what was written in his books.

• • • •

WHO WERE THE HYKSOS

• • • •

THIS IS A VERY GOOD question and no one really knows who exactly they were. It has been said that they were a Semitic people who had found their way to Egypt and got as far as Avaris (#14).

• • • •

OTHERS HAVE SAID THAT the Hyksos were a near eastern people or from Asia but the existing documentation does not really go into detail as to their exact origin (#15).

• • • •

THERE IS EVEN TROUBLE trying to find the meaning behind the name Hyksos. Some people call it an incorrect translation as they disagree with the shepherd kings definition and prefer the one that accompanies the words hikau khausut which means rulers of foreign lands (#16).

• • • •

THERE MAY SOME CONFUSION at work as Manetho was writing centuries after the fact. He may have got his data mixed up either by accident or on purpose. This confusion has had scholars attaching the name Hyksos to the Hebrews who were in the land with the ones who were said to have ruled the land between the 13th and 17th dynasties. The key to remember is that Hyksos came to Egypt from mysterious origins and left the country to a mysterious fate.

• • • •

WHICH LEAVES THE OPENING that the Hyksos could have been the Amalekites who were a people who were described as one of the first nations rendering their origin unknown and who died out from history a few centuries later without any records about their civilization left extant.

• • • •

THIS DESTRUCTION OF any knowledge falls in line with what God said he would do to the Amalekites after their attack on Israel in Exodus 17. In verse 14 God told Moses- "14 Then the Lord said to Moses, "Write this in a book as a memorial and recite it to Joshua,

that I will utterly blot out the memory of Amalek from under heaven"
(NASB).

• • • •

IF THIS IS THE CASE, the Amalekites could easily have gone to
Egypt after their battle with the Hebrews and took over the land as far
as Avaris without striking a blow. There was no one left to stop them
from doing that.

• • • •

THE PHARAOH WHO DID not know Joseph

• • • •

SINCE THE BIBLE DOES not mention the name of the Pharaoh
who took over after Joseph died many theories abound. One respected
archaeologist has said that the only time the Hebrews could have been
in Egypt and built Pithom was during the claimed Hyksos time (#17).

• • • •

THE REASONING BEHIND that identification was that the new
Hyksos king would have no real knowledge of Egyptian history and
would not have been told about Joseph and his achievements (#18).

• • • •

THAT IS HARD TO ASCERTAIN as it does not fit in with what
the Pharaoh had said when he declared that the Hebrews were to be
made slave. Another theory also pins the enslavement on the Hyksos
as the person creating this theory stated that this was something the
Egyptians would not say and it was something that the Hyksos would
say (#19).

• • • •

THAT EXPLANATION MAKES no sense as the Hyksos were trying to rule a large group of people already. Most likely the Egyptians outnumbered the Hyksos and with the latter not conquering the whole land, there were far too many free Egyptians to worry about than the Hebrews.

• • • •

THE EGYPTIANS ON THE other hand had something to fear from the growing number of Hebrews as they had, like every other ancient civilizations, reason to believe that the Hebrews would join forces with their enemies and conquer the land.

• • • •

IF THE HEBREWS WERE under Hyksos control, then they could have easily escaped to the free part of Egypt and joined forces with the Egyptians and drive out the invaders. With the Egyptians as the ones who enslaved the Hebrews, that hope and possibility disappears as the Hebrews had no place to escape to.

• • • •

TO FIND THE PHARAOH of the Exodus, it it may be left to a search of one who was not a first born child unless the Pharaoh was spared from being killed in the last plague. The Pharaoh who took over for the one killed at the Red Sea could not be a first born child.

• • • •

AS THE BIBLE TELLS us- "4 Moses said, "Thus says the Lord, 'About midnight I am going out into the midst of Egypt, 5 and all the firstborn in the land of Egypt shall die, from the firstborn of the Pharaoh who sits on his throne, even to the firstborn of the slave girl who is behind the millstones; all the firstborn of the cattle as well." (Exodus 11 NASB).

· · · ·

IT IS ALSO POSSIBLE that the Pharaoh who enslaved the Hebrews was not the same as the pharaoh of the Exodus for this reason- " 19 Now the Lord said to Moses in Midian, "Go back to Egypt, for all the men who were seeking your life are dead." (Exodus 4 NASB).

· · · ·

IT IS HARD TO SAY BUT that seems to be the indication. In finding the identity we have the clues just as we have the clues as to when the Hyksos ruled in Egypt and who the Hyksos were.

· · · ·

THE EGYPTIAN TIMELINE cannot be left up to unbelieving Egyptologists to figure out. They are not in search of the truth and may still be carrying out the ancient Egyptian tradition of creating a history that makes their people look better than they were. They also do not have God helping them.

· · · ·

WORKS CITED

· · · ·

#1. REDMOUNT, C. A. (2001). Ethnicity, Pottery, and the Hyksos at Tell El-Maskhuta in the Egyptian Delta. Biblical Archaeologist: Volume 58 1-4, (electronic ed.), 183.

#2. Wood, B., (2016), 'DAVID ROHL'S REVISED EGYPTIAN CHRONOLOGY: A VIEW FROM PALESTINE", Biblia.work, https://www.biblia.work/sermons/davidrohls-revised-egyptian-chronology-a-view-from-palestine/

#3. Malik, J., (2011), "Egyptian Art", Phaidon, Pg. 430

#4. Harrison, R.K., (2005), "Old Testament Times", Baker Books

#5. Lundstrom, P., (2020), "The Royal Code of Turin", Pharaoh.se, https://pharaoh.se/royal-canon-of-turin

#6. Ibid

#7. Ibid

#8. Kinnaer, J., (2018), " Manetho", The Egyptian Site, http://ancient-egypt.org/who-is-who/m/manetho.html

#9. Manetho. (1964). History of Egypt and Other Works. (T. E. Page, E. Capps, L. A. Post, W. H. D. Rouse, & E. H. Warmington, Eds., W. G. Waddell, Trans.) (p. vii). Cambridge, MA; London: Harvard University Press; William Heinemann Ltd.

#10. Ibid

#11 ABR, (2005). Bible and Spade, 18(1), 9.

#12 Dunn, J., (2020), " Who were the Hyksos", Tour Egypt, http://www.touregypt.net/featurestories/hyksos.htm

#13 Op Cit Kinnaer (2018)

#14 Mark, J., (2017), "Hyksos", Ancient History Encyclopedia, https://www.ancient.eu/Hyksos/

#15 Youngblood, R. F., Bruce, F. F., & Harrison, R. K., Thomas Nelson Publishers (Eds.). (1995). In Nelson's new illustrated Bible dictionary. Nashville, TN: Thomas Nelson, Inc.

#16 Op Cit Dunn (2020)

#17 Wood, B., (2008), "From Ramesses to Shiloh: Archaeological Discoveries Bearing on the Exodus-Judges Period", Associates for Biblical Research, https://biblearchaeology.org/research/conquest-of-canaan/2403-from-ramesses-to-shiloh-archaeological-discoveries-bearing-on-the-exodusjudges-period?highlight=WyJoeWtzb3MiLCInaHlrc29zJyIsIidoeWtzb3MnLXF

#18 Ibid

#19 EU, (2020), "Date of the Exodus", Evidence Unseen, http://www.evidenceunseen.com/date-of-the-exodus/

The Ipuwer Papyrus & the Christian

MANY PEOPLE DO NOT care

. . . . .

WHEN IT COMES TO HISTORY and archaeology there is a lack of caring about what the ancients did and when they wrote their masterful works. These people have a lot more on their minds than what ancient people put down on 'paper'.

. . . . .

WHETHER THEY ADMIT to it or not, the Ipuwer Papyrus and a large majority of history impacts their faith, if they have one, in Jesus. If left to the unbelieving world, much of the Old Testament and foundation for the New is lost, replaced by ideas heavily influenced by unbelief.

. . . . .

THAT CANNOT TAKE PLACE as the truth cannot be hid even if the truth offends many unbelievers and keeps them from converting and taking Jesus as their Savior. The story about the Ipuwer Papyrus cannot remain in the hands of the unbeliever.

. . . . .

WHAT IS THE IPUWER Papyrus

. . . . .

ONE OF THE MOST INTERESTING aspects of the Ipuwer Papyrus is that it is recorded on the Papyrus Leiden 344 and it contains information that resembles the different plagues that God sent to afflict the Egyptian people (#1).

• • • •

THIS IS WHAT CAUSES the controversy as there is so little physical evidence to support the biblical era that records the Hebrew sojourn in Egypt. Having this piece of ancient physical evidence would go along ways to proving the Bible true.

• • • •

ONE OF THE PROBLEMS that keep this piece of ancient Egyptian literature from being accepted as an account of the pre-Exodus trouble is that most scholars do not date the contents to the time of the Exodus even though the papyrus it was written on dates to about the 13th century BC. The contents are dated to between 2000 & 1700 BC (#2).

• • • •

WHY IS THERE CONTROVERSY

• • • •

ONE OF THE MAIN REASONS why there is any controversy at all about the contents of this document is that the majority of scholars do not believe there was an actual Exodus from Egypt by the Hebrew people. That disbelief naturally influences their view on the Ipuwer Papyrus (#3).

• • • •

THIS ATTITUDE IS AN important one as unbelief tends to blind the eyes of scholars to the truth. This means that their dating of the document even though it is written on Exodus era, give or take 100 years, parchment is suspect.

• • • •

BUT THERE HAVE BEEN scholars over the decades that have disagreed with such an early date of the contents. Most do not like being mentioned in the same sentence as Immanuel Velikovsky and have omitted his name from some of their works when those contents agree with the controversial historian. He stated that the Ipuwer Papyrus was written by someone who experienced the plagues and saw the Exodus take place (#4).

• • • • •

IT DOES NOT READ LIKE someone was creating a scary bed time tale or a fairy tale in the likes of Hans Christian Anderson or Aseop. The Papyrus has the feel of an actual event thus it must be treated as a true story based on an actual event. Which is what Velikovsky also determined as did Von Seter (#5).

• • • • •

WHY THE EARLY DATING

• • • •

THIS IS HARD TO EXPLAIN as there is no real reason for why the contents were pushed back between 400 and 300 years. The papyrus itself comes from the New Kingdom era, 1550 to 1070 BC, but for some reasons the contents are given a Middle Kingdom date, approx., 1885 to 1773 BC (#6).

• • • •

THIS IS CLOSE TO WHAT other scholars have concluded as the correct time of the writing of the contents. One scholar has stated that this contents should be placed in the First Intermediate Era which dates to about 2123 to 2040 BC. (#7).

• • • •

THE ONLY PROBLEM WITH these early dates is that there is no real historical record depicting of such a similar calamity to befall Egypt. If there was the many scholars who talk about the early dating of the contents could produce the historical record, the manuscript detailing such an invasion and so on. None have and none exist.

·····

YET THAT DOESN'T STOP scholars pointing to the large gap between the events described in the Papyrus and the book of Exodus. They go as far as stating that the two records are not depicting actual historical events (#8).

·····

THIS RANDOM CATEGORIZING of historical events is what is to be expected from those who do not accept the Bible as true. If they do not believe the Exodus is true why would they believe that any evidence for it exists or is even true?

·····

THIS IS WHAT MESSES up people's faith when they listen to these unbelieving scholars and accept their opinion of God's word.

·····

WHO WAS IPUWER

·····

THIS IS ANOTHER POINT against the early dating of the papyrus bearing his name. It is not li9ke he did not exist. What is not known is which Ipuwer is the author. His name or title is found in the Old, Middle and New Kingdoms. In fact, his name appears in a 19th

Dynasty tomb. These are not the only pieces of physical evidence that remain for this or some other Ipuwer (#9).

. . . .

IT SHOULD BE POINTED out that since this 13th century papyrus is the only copy available it cannot be determined to be a copy of an earlier document. There is no reason that a copy should be made. What purpose would it serve?

. . . .

AT LEAST WITH MANETHO we know he was commissioned to write his histories of Egypt but no such information is found for Ipuwer. It is possible that he recorded it for posterity so that everyone would know that the Egyptians endured a terrible storm of plagues, etc.

. . . .

WITH THE ANCIENT EGYPTIAN reputation of altering their history, it is no wonder corroboration is not found in official ancient government records. Nothing stops ordinary Egyptian citizens from recording what took place so their family would know the truth about their history (#10).

. . . .

THE CRITERIA USED TO determine the actual date

. . . .

ONE OF THE MAIN CRITERIA that is used to determine the date of any manuscript is the writing style or the genre often applied by modern scholars according to modern definitions. Yet these different writing styles are not exclusive to the dynasty to which they are credited (#11).

. . . .

PEOPLE, EVEN ANCIENT Egyptians, are free to write in any style they want no matter what era, Kingdom or decade they happen to reside. This literary criteria is more of a straw man argument than actual fact. Many manuscripts have probably been misdated because of the accepted methods of classification.

. . . .

MODERN SCHOLARS DO this with the Pauline Epistles trying to down grade his words to fake rather than genuine writing. It is no wonder that they would do it to the Ipuwer Papyrus as the unbeliever does not want to give credibility to the biblical record.

. . . .

THERE IS NOTHING ELSE to help date the contents to a previous Kingdom or back up to 400 years in history. The fact that it is considered a poem doe snot render the contents to an earlier date nor to the realms of fiction. Even poems can relate the truth and record actual events of a cataclysm (#12).

. . . .

WHAT THE EXISTENCE of this Papyrus does prove is twofold. One, as Kenneth Kitchen has said, the Exodus account and the Ipuwer Papyrus speak about the same topic. Two, the Exodus remained in the minds of the Egyptians for centuries after the fact (#13).

. . . .

IN OTHER WORDS, THE writer of the document considered the events real and wanted them recorded for whatever reason he may have had. It is possible that the author recorded those events because he was in opposition to the ancient Egyptian habit of altering their history.

. . . .

WHAT IS THE TRUTH

. . . .

ONE OF THE PROBLEMS with dating an ancient document is that the date given to those documents are based on what the scholar believes, not what is true. Given the close relationship to the Biblical Exodus the bias against the Bible is a powerful influence that leads scholars to misdate important physical evidence like the Ipuwer Papyrus.

. . . .

THERE IS NO REASON to date it earlier than the Exodus. Because there is no historical event prior to the plagues and the Exodus that would inspire someone to record those traumatic events.

. . . .

SCHOLARS HAVE TRIED to place the writing to the accepted Hyksos invasion of Egypt in the 1700 BC and onward but without success (#14). The Hyksos probably arrived after the Exodus when Egypt was at its weakest point ever in its history save for when its people arrived in the area after the Babel Diaspora. They were not the cause of the Exodus or the plagues but the end result after the cataclysm finished its work on the Egyptian people.

. . . .

THERE IS NOTHING TO support any conclusion other than the fact that this document records the plagues prior to the Exodus. The Ipuwer Papyrus is extra biblical support for that biblical event and shows that they Bible is true.

• • • •

WORKS CITED

• • • •

#1. BLEDSOE, S. (2016). Egyptian Literature. In J. D. Barry, D. Bomar, D. R. Brown, R. Klippenstein, D. Mangum, C. Sinclair Wolcott, ... W. Widder (Eds.), The Lexham Bible Dictionary. Bellingham, WA: Lexham Press.

#2. Ibid

#3. Habermehl, A. 2018. The Ipuwer Papyrus and the Exodus. In Proceedings of the Eighth International Conference on Creationism, ed.J.H. Whitmore, pp. 1–6. Pittsburgh, Pennsylvania: Creation Science Fellowship https://pdfs.semanticscholar.org/4b1d/4f6874ab5e24509d2d307cc7185aac9651e6.pdf

#4. MP, (2020), "THE PAPYRUS IPUWER", Mikamar Publishing, http://www.mikamar.biz/Pensee%20III/3-13-papyrus-ipuwer.htm

#5. Ibid

#6. Sutherland, A., (2017), "Is Ipuwer Papyrus A Report Of An Ancient Catastrophe?", Ancient Pages, http://www.ancientpages.com/2017/08/07/ipuwer-papyrus-report-ancient-catastrophe/

#7. Murnane William J. (2001). Review of First Civilizations: Ancient Mesopotamia and Egypt by Robert Chadwick. Biblical Archaeologist: Volume 60 1-4, (electronic ed.), 187.

#8. Kennedy, T. M. (2016). Egypt, Plagues of. In J. D. Barry, D. Bomar, D. R. Brown, R. Klippenstein, D. Mangum, C. Sinclair Wolcott, ... W. Widder (Eds.), The Lexham Bible Dictionary. Bellingham, WA: Lexham Press.

#9. Op Cit Habermehl, A. 2018

#10 Ibid

#11. Op Cit Bledsoe (2016)

#12. Graves, D.E., (2014), "Bonus 29 - Ipuwer Papyrus", Biblical Archaeology,   https://biblicalarchaeologygraves.blogspot.com/2014/12/bonus-29-ipuwer-papyrus.html

#13. Ibid

#14. (2001). Biblical Archaeologist 1-4, 36(electronic ed.).

SOME YEARS AGO AS I was browsing through a bookstore in Korea I came across a book by Dr. Erwin Lutzer. It was called Hitler's Cross: How the Cross was used to promote the Nazi agenda. When I saw the name of the author and the title of the book the first thought I had was now I was going to get the truth on the subject.

• • • •

UNFORTUNATELY, I WAS wrong and the book did not deliver what I had hoped. Instead the subject matter was not dealt with very carefully, thoroughly or even academically. The reader was given chapter after chapter of the gospel message and that is what I remember of that book.

• • • •

NO POINT MADE BY DR. Lutzer was compelling, accurate or even close to why Hitler used the cross. I was told later that the reason Christian authors are putting the gospel message in their works to Christian readers is that Ken Ham of AIG said one cannot divorce the topic from the gospel.

• • • •

NOW I LIKE A LOT OF what Ken Ham writes and I enjoy a lot of what AIG produces but in this case one has to disagree with this thinking as one does not need to preach the gospel message to those who already believe.

• • • •

IT IS CALLED PREACHING to the choir and that is not something Jesus taught in Scripture. In fact when Jesus confronted Peter, he told his apostle to 'feed his sheep' (john 21:15 to 17) One is not feeding Jesus' sheep by keeping them at square one and only giving them the gospel message to grow on.

. . . . .

JESUS' WORDS WERE SUPPORTED later by Paul who said talked about growing in spiritual maturity in 1 Corinthians 13:11. One cannot speak like an adult when they are treated like a child by the leaders of the church. It is a responsibility of the church leader to help their people grow strong in Jesus and the word.

. . . . .

THE BELIEVER NEEDS to learn how to handle their faith, withstand evil and be a strong warrior for Christ. But they cannot achieve what God wants them to be when they are deprived of the spiritual food they need to grow big and strong spiritually.

. . . . .

THE CHURCH MEMBER HAS to get past square one and build on the gospel they believed for salvation. The continued feeding of the gospel to those who already believe will be detrimental to their spiritual growth.

. . . . .

AND IF BIBLICAL ARCHAEOLOGY is going to have a future then the biblical archaeologist must learn how use what they know and to feed the people of the church correctly. Jesus' command to Peter is not just for biblical texts but also for all subjects.

. . . . .

THIS IS NOT AN EASY task but it is the only way that Biblical Archaeology can remain relevant to the lives of the church goer. While the believer in the church may not go off on archaeological digs or participate in academic discussions, they can use the information fed them by the biblical archaeologist in many ways.

• • • •

THEY CAN US THAT INFORMATION to teach their children the truth, help them understand the Bible and give them ammunition when their faith and their Bible comes under attack. In other words, they will not become a fallen believer when an unbeliever 'proves' their Bible is not true.

• • • •

IT IS THE RESPONSIBILITY of the biblical archaeologist to transmit their knowledge to the believer in a way that the latter will understand and then realize how vital that data is to their and their family's faith.

• • • •

GOD HAS CALLED BIBLICAL archaeologists to a special task and it is not just to keep the unbeliever honest. It is also to protect the faithful by giving them the information they need ton a daily basis.

• • • •

BIBLICAL ARCHAEOLOGY has an important role in the church, its existence and in its fight against evil. It is not superior to other topics nor is it inferior to them either. It needs to be heard in the proper manner so that Sunday School teachers have the truth and can pass it on to their young charges in a way that will help strengthen the class member's faith.

• • • •

ONE WAY TO BORE A CHURCH member, a reader or a listener is to feed them the same information over and over. Ken Ham has written on how the young people of the church have lost their faith when they went off to college.

• • • •

THIS IS HOW WE PREVENT that drop off rate from getting greater. We start feeding them the correct information when they are young. So by the time they are college age they are prepared to face what will come when they leave the security of their parent's home and their church.

• • • •

AS THESE YOUNG PEOPLE are taught, they are also given lessons on how to use their new found information properly. One of the major complaints made by atheists is that the Christian is uneducated and does not know their Bible.

• • • •

THE BIBLICAL ARCHAEOLOGIST can help change all of that by getting the right material to the pastors, church leaders, and Sunday school teachers. They in turn teach it correctly to their congregations.

• • • •

PROTECTING THE BELIEVER is not found in isolating them from the world and its thinking. Protecting the believer, no matter their age, comes by giving them the right information that helps them grow in their faith and become mature, strong Christians.

• • • •

THE MILITARY UNITS of different nations do not get great soldiers by telling them the same thing over and over. Those soldiers are not told their oaths after every meeting, every lecture and in every manual. Military personal are trained correctly and given information to help them become better soldiers and so on.

· · · ·

THEY ARE GIVEN NEW information that will help them in battle, new techniques of hand to hand fighting. And on it goes. They are not kept at square one. Their entry into the military is built upon till they become good military personal.

· · · ·

SADLY, THE CHURCH DOES not do this and too many church members are left vulnerable for evil to destroy. Biblical archaeology information does not supplant theological or spiritual teaching. It works hand in hand with it helping to get to the truth the right way.

· · · ·

IT IS AN AID THAT HELPS people understand what God is saying in the Bible. Biblical Archaeology does not bring new revelation, it helps clarify the information God recorded in the Bible and shows that his word, even the parts without physical evidence, are true to the last letter.

· · · ·

BUILDING THE FAITH of the believer is not the sole task of the pastor of the church. Evangelism is not the sole task of those called to be evangelists. The biblical archaeologist plays a key role in both areas with hen he or she communicates the truth to the people of the church.

· · · ·

PLANTING SEEDS IS JUST the first step in evangelism and those seeds can come from the truth that the Biblical archaeologist digs up through his or her research. Watering the seed is the next step and the same holds true here for the biblical archaeologist.

. . . . .

EVEN THOUGH THEY ARE not pastors or evangelists, the biblical archaeologist can make a great contribution to the church. But only if they are following the spirit of truth to the truth.

. . . . .

IT TAKES A LOT OF WORK to get to the truth and sometimes like Dr. Lutzer Christian authors do not cover the ground very well. The biblical archaeologist has to ask God to guide them to the truth when they read non christian works.

. . . . .

SOMETIMES, THE EVIDENCE or information the biblical archaeologist needs can only come through non Christian archaeologists because other Christians have failed in their duty to cover the subject as they should.

. . . . .

GETTING THE WHOLE STORY is important because that is the only way to get to the truth. The biblical archaeologist needs God's help to wind their way through the maze of non Christian thinking.

. . . . .

AS THEY DO THAT, THEY also need to ask God to show them how to refute the unbelieving archaeologist and their theories. They are not going to do it on their own. With God nothing is impossible and feeding the church correctly and getting them to be mature Christians takes the help of God.

· · · ·

TO BE A GOOD BIBLICAL archaeologist one has to use their own faith knowing that God will lead them to the truth. Then they have to have faith that God will give them an audience so that his people will grow strong in their faith.

· · · ·

ONE CANNOT ASSUME THEY have the truth. They must know the truth and know that they have found it. When they do, they build upon their faith in order to build the faith of other believers.

· · · ·

BIBLICAL ARCHAEOLOGY has a role in the church. It just has to be done correctly for the church to benefit.

Addendum

Who Wrote The Bible

· · · ·

OVER THE YEARS AND through many a discussions on spiritual matters with non-believers, the sentence, 'I do not believe a bronze Age book written by a bunch of goat herders' has been spoken in a variety of ways. All those ways were meant to insult God's divine and Holy book.

· · · ·

AFTER A WHILE IT GOT me thinking and the idea to list the humans involved in penning the physical scriptures (God wrote it but used humans to pen the actual words for human eyes). We can first dispense with the idea that the Bible was written during one era of archaeological time (Bronze Age). The Bible was written over 1,000+ years covering more than one archaeological era.

· · · ·

IT IS NOT A PRODUCT of the Bronze Age, in fact, we can dismiss the three age system altogether as that was an arbitrary division to meet a demand in a museum showing a couple of hundred years ago. The world did not progress as archaeology defines it, as we know that even today in the supposed Nuclear Age there are still stone age people in existence and thriving in their corner of the world.

· · · ·

WHAT ABOUT THE MEN whom God used to put His words onto terrestrial paper. Here is a short sketch of the men with the books they wrote listed first:

• • • •

#1.   GENESIS,   EXODUS,   Leviticus,   Numbers   &
Deuteronomy–Moses- a former prince, educated in the court of the
Egyptian Pharaoh, part-time herder in Midian, leader of the people of
Israel.

• • • •

#2. JOSHUA– JOSHUA- military man, spy, successor to Moses,
Conqueror.

• • • •

#3. JUDGES– JEWISH TALMUD says Samuel wrote this book- Was
a judge of Israel and a prophet of God.

• • • •

#4. RUTH– UNKNOWN.

• • • •

#5. 1 & 2 SAMUEL–THE Jewish Talmud states Samuel wrote these
books- Was a judge of Israel and a Prophet of God.

• • • •

#6. 1 & 2 KINGS–UNKNOWN.
     #7. 1 & 2 Chronicles– The Jewish Talmud says Ezra wrote these
books-Priest.

• • • •

#8. EZRA– EZRA-PRIEST

• • • •

#9. NEHEMIAH– POSSIBLY Ezra-Priest; {if it was Nehemiah he was a King's cup bearer}.

#10 Esther–unknown.

#11 Job– unknown, Jewish tradition says it was Moses but not confirmed.

. . . . .

#12 PSALMS–DAVID- SHEPHERD boy, warrior, King of Israel.

. . . . .

#13 PROVERBS, ECCLESIASTES & Song of Songs–Most likely Solomon–prince, King of Israel.

. . . . .

#14 ISAIAH–ISAIAH-PROPHET of God.

. . . . .

#15 JEREMIAH & POSSIBLY Lamentations–Jeremiah–Prophet of God.

. . . . .

#16 EZEKIEL– EZEKIEL- Prophet of God.

#17 Daniel–most likely Daniel-Possibly from the royal family or the nobility (Dan. 1:3, 8), served in the Babylonian King's court, educated again by the Babylonian King's men (Dan. 1:4-7).

. . . . .

#18 HOSEA–HOSEA- PROPHET of God.

. . . . .

#19 JOEL–JOEL-PROPHET of God.

• • • •

#20 AMOS–AMOS- PROPHET of God, shepherd and farmer.

• • • •

#21 JONAH–JONAH- PROPHET of God.

• • • •

#22 MICAH– MICAH- PROPHET of God.
#23 Nahum– Nahum- Prophet of God.

• • • •

#24 HABAKKUK– HABAKKUK- Prophet of God.

• • • •

#25 ZEPHANIAH– ZEPHANIAH- Prophet of God, descendant of King Hezekiah.

• • • •

#26 HAGGAI– HAGGAI- PROPHET of God.

• • • •

#27 ZECHARIAH– ZECHARIAH- Prophet of God.

• • • •

#28 MALACHI– MALACHI– Prophet of God.

• • • •

#29 MATTHEW– MATTHEW- Tax Collector, apostle of Jesus.

• • • •

#30 MARK– MARK–ASSOCIATE of the apostle Peter.

• • • •

#31 LUKE & ACTS– LUKE- Doctor.

• • • •

#32 JOHN, 1ST, 2ND, 3RD John & Revelation–John- Fisherman, apostle of Jesus

• • • •

#33 ROMANS, 1 & 2 CORINTHIANS, Galatians, Ephesians, Philippians, Colossians, 1 & 2 Thess., 1 & 2 Timothy, Titus & Philemon– Paul- trained rabbi, very well-educated, missionary for Jesus.

• • • •

#34 HEBREWS– UNKNOWN.

• • • •

#35 JAMES–TOO MANY MEN named James associated with Jesus to be sure (if it were Jesus' brother then we could say carpenter having learned the trade from his father Joseph).

• • • •

#36 1ST & 2ND PETER– Peter–Apostle and fisherman.

• • • •

#37 JUDE– JUDE- OCCUPATION unknown (if it was Jesus' brother then we could say carpenter).

• • • •

AS YOU CAN SEE VERY few of the authors of the books of the Bible were sheep or goat herders. 3 in total and two were raised up by God to lead His people. The real authorship of the Bible belongs to God and who the men God used to pen the physical words were is irrelevant.

· · · ·

IRRELEVANT BECAUSE the Bible is not a human book and the men involved are not important except that they obeyed God and listened to the Spirit of God and wrote what they were told to write. Their source would have been God who would have all the details of every conversation, every act, every life and could produce those details found in the Bible without a problem.

· · · ·

THIS IS WHY WE CAN say that Moses could write about Adam and Eve without human sources because God supplied Him the details. The biblical writers did not need to use human works but probably were led in some instances to do so as Luke said he researched all things that he wrote. Of course, he would have had the Holy Spirit guiding his research in order to get to the truth and then had help writing the words down as we have them.

· · · ·

THE MEN GOD USED CAME from a variety of backgrounds and employment, men prepared to do a specific job God wanted them to do. In most of the cases we do not know how educated they were but then with God doing the writing and providing the help they did not have to be. God uses anyone who is willing to obey. Being highly educated is not a prerequisite nor is God using uneducated men justification to ignore learning.

· · · ·

THE CHARGES THAT THE bible is a human product written by sheep herders or priests with an agenda during the Bronze Age are very unfounded and can easily be turned aside when one looks for and uses the truth.